TEACHER! TEACHER!

by

Ed Miller

Gotham Books

30 N Gould St.
Ste. 20820, Sheridan, WY 82801
https://gothambooksinc.com/

Phone: 1 (307) 464-7800

© 2024 *Ed Miller.* All rights reserved.

No part of this book may be reproduced, stored in a retrieval system, or transmitted by any means without the written permission of the author.

Published by Gotham Books (January 26, 2024)

ISBN: 979-8-88775-837-4 (P)
ISBN: 979-8-88775-838-1 (E)

Because of the dynamic nature of the Internet, any web addresses or links contained in this book may have changed since publication and may no longer be valid.

The views expressed in this work are solely those of the author and do not necessarily reflect the views of the publisher, and the publisher hereby disclaims any responsibility for them.

This compilation was created because the material herein was found purely by accident when exhuming material to be disposed of something one might call clutter. Obviously, the letters from my file were a complete revelation. Some of the literature was written before it was connected to any book, having been done for a creative writing class and in some cases complete fiction. The photographs are from the school collection of pictures saved from non-use in publications.

This book has not been edited by a professional. Excuse any typos.

ACKNOWLEDGEMENT

First is TIME and FATE. Time which has given me 90 years of an amazing life, and fate which has prevented me from a lifelong occupation as an optician, painter or waiter, instead of a career as an art teacher. Thanks, must be given to my mother-in-law, for promoting my return to college after a long hiatus. For my wife's moral and economic support, working throughout my college years and typing my papers and reports. All the supervisors at Linden who encouraged me, as is evident in these files and all the anecdotes that my UFT creative writing class provided support and approval of all these retirement years. Mostly, the gift of a brilliant student body, whose endeavor earns them my eternal gratitude and recognition evermore.

Art Teacher/Coordinator

PREFACE

This school photo has little relation to the person writing this collection of stories, photographs, and reproductions of students' masterful art work. In more than 35 years since this experience were lived, mostly joyful,

I cannot say that the accuracy can be verified, or the names recalled correctly, except on the documents. It was absolutely serendipitous how I came across the envelope containing the treasure trove of files that my supervisors amassed crediting me with accomplishments long forgotten.

Likewise, was the magnificent collection of artworks found that was stored all these years, in addition to the gifts that adorn the walls of my apartment. Therefore, dear reader, please understand that this labor of love is meant to be shared, some highlights of a 20 year journey at The Linden School, in St. Albans, Queens, that happened due to circumstances beyond my control, much as most of my life experiences have been.

Ed Miller, Retiree 2015

Table of Contents

ACKNOWLEDGEMENT iv

PREFACE vi

Of Ventures and Vetoes 1

Junk and Treasure 10

Don Quixote 14

Found Object Sculpture 16

Crisis Management 19

Extra-Curricular 24

Like The Bible 28

Dilemma 31

Templates 34

Sample Of Creativity Using Templates 38

The Bureau 42

Student Teacher 48

The Observation 52

Hallway Crises 56

Deal 59

Teacher Teacher! 63

Crayons, Crisis, Creativity 68

Another Crisis 70

Mr. Tag Along 71

Surprise 80

Surprise, Surprise 82

Je Comprende 83

Need To Know 85

The Little Drummer Boy 91

Becomes of a Tuba 97

The End Term Party 108

The Reunion 111

Approval? 117

GIFT ART 119

LIZA AND LISA 123

In Closing 127

IN CONCLUSION 129

Of Ventures and Vetoes

My appointment to teach at Linden Junior High School was an adventure of immense proportions. Actually, it had a built-in end because I was a temporary replacement for a woman who was on her sabbatical leave. The Board of Ed presented me with two guide books, which I was supposed to follow to the letter. My being an iconoclast in my thinking and acting, the books were placed on my coat-closet shelf, where they remained until I turned them in twenty years later, upon my retirement. The other oddity was that in addition to teaching, the position I was assigned was as art coordinator, in charge of ordering and distributing the art supplies to the other five art teachers and to act as conduit with the district. The Assistant Principal, Mr. Gaston, appreciated my maturity and wisdom in the performance of these responsibilities and it gave me great freedom and discretion in that job.

The teacher in charge of designing the teacher's class schedules, accepted the idea that for shop classes, band, Home Eco and art classes, it would make sense having two periods in tandem rather than the ordinary one period arrangement of the academic classes. This would eliminate duplication of arrival time, attendance, distribution of materials etc. and gave more to activity time. Another part of the plan was to give the choice of special classes to the students. The motivation for success on the student's part apparent it was under these circumstances that I found my students were eager and interested in the expression of creative art in my class. When the drawing skills became apparent in the classroom, I decided to give the children a real opportunity. I prepared heavy cardboard, cut clipboard size, on which to attach drawing paper. The fall weather was ideal, for no outerwear was necessary and we left the confines of the building to sit and sketch the outdoor scenes in front of the school. Troes, cars and houses were great subjects The children were amazing! Their drawings were amazing! For 7th graders them attitude was amazing! The art work and the artists were photographed by me and remain part of my archives. So why was there an order to discontinue this program? The AP was apologetic, despite the fact that he was very pleased with the results.

The operative word was, "INSURANCE. The principal was sorry, too, but it was Bd of Ed. policy that prohibited such activity off school grounds without prior approval. So the successful drawing project had to be scrapped because of the VETO!

I was dismayed but not cowed. My art room windows looked out on the school playground, which was used in the good weather by the Phys. Ed classes. It seemed that it was also available by the local families on weekends for play and pleasure. Beside the sports games, basketball, baseball etc., there were benches and stones tables for chess and checker players. Wonderful, I thought. If the Plys Bd. department could use the park, why not the art department. No insurance problem.

At the next opportunity, my art students found the tables and benches perfect for their drawing program and the ball players, perfect models AMAZING! Well, until the gym teachers complained that it interfered with their athletic program. Some of the art students, having completed their assignment decided to join in the basketball game. The next thing I knew was a talk with the A.P., who sympathized with me but the Phys. Ed. department had more clout and the VETO was again instituted.

Undaunted, I was determined to give these terrific kids opportunities commensurate with their talent and imagination. In the Bd of Ed. supply catalogue, I found that plaster of paris on gauze, supposedly for use as casts in case of bone fracture, would suit my purpose in teaching sculpting. There were also available basins in which to soak the gauze. When I asked the children to bring in old newspapers, they were a little surprised but true to my expectation, they provided enough to cover the double tables and to make paper mache. The double tables were pushed together so four children could share one basin.

Step one, drawing a figure of an animal or person, was followed by making a foundation of paper mache. Time was allowed to set the preliminary work in the cabinets under the window sills. The sliding doors were left open so the work could dry and harden before the next class. The drawings helped identify the foundation work. I never saw such eager children when it came to clean-up time. One would never suspect what had been happening minutes before, thanks to busy hands and paper toweling.

Several students couldn't wait until the next class so they came by to check on their pieces So eager were they to get back to their project that my previous class had hardly left the room before the 7th graders were rushing in. Newspapers were spread, basins were half filled with water and all were ready by the time attendance was taken. I had to take some time to explain the technique of applying the plaster-of-paris gauze which I had cut into three inch strips. This was different than using paper strips because the plaster was harder to manipulate. It became apparent that having a partner help became a wise choice. Hands full of plaster, faces decorated with the white goo access not as assured as expected but when clean-up time came, not everyone was ready. I allowed those who needed a few minutes more to stay and finish, giving them a pass excusing their lateness to the next class.

Again, the drying process had to take place What was different was that there was an apparent sculptural form being created. The big surprise came the following week when I showed them my sample piece completely covered in gold paint. First, they had to be sure the piece was stable, could stand on its own and being three dimensional, be seen from all sides. They had to be patient because there was only one special soft brush to paint the gold with. Again, partners worked together to carefully turn the piece as the gold was applied. With much care each work had to be placed in the cabinet to dry. Although most of the pieces worked, some did not. That child's unhappiness was expected. A short discussion about abstract art made even the less successful a work of art.

Then came the VETO #3. The head custodian, during the after-school rounds, noticed some white residue in the sink. When he asked me what it was, I explained the project and showed him the beautiful work. He, in as kindly a way as possible explained the hazard of clogging the school's drainage system with plaster and asked me to henceforth advise him of the materials that I planned to use. Before the next class meeting, I removed each piece and set it atop the cabinet for photographing. The set of Polaroid pictures of the work is one of my treasures. The art show-case assigned to me, put their work on display until the end of the year when the students could choose to take them home.

At a different time and a different class, the motivating discussion was African Masks. The students prepared short essays about Voodoo and other forms of worship on the continent. After consulting with the custodian, I was able to get powdered clay to mold the base for the masks. This time he provided me with two ten gallon plastic cans into which the residue was placed for disposal. The sink and the plumbing were spared.

The students were given the option of designing their own mask, it's size, shape and colors Again, the desks were set up for four children to share a common source of water for mixing the clay and the tools needed to model the piece. Double periods were essential for any such project. Fortunately, there was no mischief during these sessions that might disrupt the program. The art supervisor came by occasionally to observe the progress, giving tacit approval. The students loved the hands-on approach to art, especially trying to creatively outdo each other. Again, patience was required between each stage of the operation. When the dried masks were readied with a coat of binder needed to make the surface of the clay nonporous, able to accept the colored acrylic paint.

The excitement and enthusiasm was quite obvious from the resulting work. When the paint had dried, a showing was held. The masks were set up along the window cabinets and the AP and Principal were invited. Each student gave a short report about the research done for the piece, what part of Africa it represented, the choice of shape, design and colors used. Again, I took Polaroid pictures of the work before it was put into the ball showcase outside my art room 212. Prior consultation avoided any veto interfering with our creative art projects.

Junk and Treasure

The cordial relationship with Mr. Readous, the chief custodian resulted in several wondrous projects. One started when Bill approached me with a problem. Someone had left a roll of brass sheeting in his supply room and he had no use of it. If I did not want it, he would junk it. As soon as it could, I picked up his junk, my treasure and designed a magnificent project for my senior art class.

"Relief Sculpture!" Some of the most important and impressive work done at the time of Michaelangelo, Leonardo and Ghiberti who made the Doors of Paradise of the baptistry in Florence, Italy. It was done in bronze relief instead of in-the-round and had religious significance. My job was to flatten this roll, smooth it and cut it into small sheet for the students to work on it. It was fortunate that I still had many of the tools from my college art classes to use.

It has never crossed my mind, when I had taken slides on my trip to Italy, that it would be a preliminary lesson to the project. I arranged for a slide projector and screen to display the work I was talking about. When the other art teachers heard of my plan, they brought in their classes and the kids had to double up in their seats. I invited the other teachers to supplement my remarks and it was an exceptional program.

The A.P., Mr. Gaston, an enthusiastic art supervisor cautioned me to get a release from the parents because of the hazard of sharp edges and work tools. This done, the actual work was begun. As in printing, the reverse image had to be applied to the sheet. Many pencil points were broken but the experience was exhilarating. The students had to be chased to their next class and many asked to come after school.

My invention of a base onto which the carving would be done without piercing the thin metal sheets, was itself phenomenal. The images that the kids created were amazing for students that age. I had little to do except encourage or console. Again, I cautioned against haste, and it paid off. In the meantime, I arrange the printing department to cut black sheets of mat board to be backing for the brass reliefs, and when they were finished and mounted, they were of masterpiece quality. Mr. Gaston was so pleased with his Art Department that had us set up a special display in the library for Open School Week.

When the parents came to my room to inquire of the children, I could hardly find the words of appreciation for their sending them to me. If the hadn't seen the exhibit, I directed them to the library. No one believed me, that the custodian was responsible for it all.

Not even Mr. Readous himself.

"An artist sees treasure in junk!" is an old saw. So when someone in my building discarded an old guitar, I found a prop of my students. I was very fortunate that many of my classes were made up of exceptionally talented children which allowed me to venture into areas reserve for much more mature artist. My collection of old wine bottles and wax fruit came in handy for their drawing and painting "still-lifes", especially at the time the movie, "Lust for Life" about VanGogh was playing in the movie theaters and still-life art became popular.

The students reveled in these opportunities with an enthusiasm far beyond my expectations. When I brought in that discarded guitar, the security guard remarked, "Mr. Miller, where are the strings?" We both laughed when I replied, "In the imagination!" At first, I used it as a part of the still-life set up. The objective was for free expression by the pupils, although that included lessons in design and structure.

Not every class was able or ready to tackle such projects but the older talent classes did very well.

One day, the class was surprised to find that I had moved my desk away from the window area to near the door. I asked them to arrange their desks in a semi-circle and had the paper monitor distributed pencils and drawing paper. Having taken the attendance, I was ready to proceed. Without another word, I jumped up on the desk, with the guitar in my hand and posed for them to draw. As usual, I had left the door open, so when the teacher passed by, he remarked at how quite the class was.

Well, not exactly! One of the boys remarked, "Mr. Harris better not see you!" The Principal seldom came up to the 2nd floor, so it was a surprise when appeared in the doorway. Saying nothing, he meandered around the room and as he left remarked, "Very Nice!"

The class erupted in laughter as I shushed them back to work. This was the first of several classes where drawing from the model took place. In one class, a student decided to volunteer to model with the guitar. He was always the "wise-guy" so when I helped him up onto the desk and gave him the guitar, he was duly surprised.

When I offered him a chair, his macho refused but he changed his mind after five minutes. He had to admit that standing, even sitting still in a pose position was not easy.

One time, I had a student take a photo of me posing and this time I took a shot of him. He became a celebrity when I submitted his picture for the school "Bulletin!" I was happy that this principal approved and did not veto the project. Although drawing from the model is a very difficult skill, the work product was very good.

I am reminded of a complaint from a science teacher that one of my students sat in his class drawing figures. I asked him, "Were they anatomically, correct?" With his reply that they were, I suggested. "Encourage him!"

Don Quixote

Marty Levine of class 7SPEI, was an exceptional kid. When the discussion period, which was part of the lesson plan was held, it was Marty who raised his hand most often. It was no surprise that when the students brought in their work, after the long holiday weekend, fulfilling the assignment to construct a piece of found object sculpture, that his really showed exceptional creativity and originality. After the children's work was set up on the teacher's desk, and set on wooden bases, it was he who was the first to volunteer to explain bis Marty began, "The teacher said, "junk!" and my pop has plenty." He went on, "We live in a one family house that belonged to my grandparents who were brought up in the 'depression.

So they didn't believe in throwing anything away and the basement was full of junk!" As soon as I got home from school, I went to the kitchen cabinet drawer and found my treasure.

"My mother wanted to know what I needed in that drawer and when I told her what the art teacher said, that the parents could help, she nearly fainted. I won't repeat exactly what she said, then but it was crazy Anyhow, I found a pair of Chinese chopsticks and a million bottle corks. "O.K. Kiddo!" she mused. "Let's see what we can do!" And I did! 1 dumped everything on the kitchen floor. Well, that's what she said! There were all kinds of stuff, green swizzle sticks, cardboard match-boxes with leftover wooden matches and some pieces of old carpeting. We had recently seen, The Man of La Mancha and like magic, there it came to us "I asked mom to break the swizzle sticks, for the legs, then she told me that parents incant lathers, too So when dud came home from work for the holiday weekend, he was included in the project. A seventh grader's hands needed help and a few suggestions did just that for instance, when I applied the Elmer's glue, Ded's strong hands held the pieces in place until the glue began to set. He even recommended my drawing the silly features on the cork face, then glue it onto the matchbox horse: My concern that there was no body had dad say.

That's what makes it a funny Don Quixote!" And, so it does." Mother agreed.

Found Object Sculpture

It was the weekend of Memorial Day and my six grade art class was anxious for a holiday away from school. The term was near its end and the level of achievement was very high. Each endeavor resulted in work above my expectation for these eleven year olds. So many projects, so much success led me to discussing Pablo Picasso's experiment in "*Objet Trouve*". The piece he had created was a goat made literally of junk.

When I proposed the students do this as a homework assignment over the holiday weekend, a murmur, a sigh and a groan came back at me. Never had these sweet kids reacted this way. My alternative was a written assignment or some kind of written test which would be a punishment for me, as well as the students. When the disquiet subsided, I went on to suggest ideas which would stir their imagination How could they not be interested in a treasure hunt from which they could construct their work. I made no restrictions nor promoted anything specific as a guideline, except that it should be original, based on what objects they had selected.

There were two exceptions the finished sculpture need not be completed that weekend and they were allowed to have their parents help. Their reaction was utter disbelief. Before the class was dismissed, several students began asking questions as to ideas they already pictured in their heads. The question arose about making a drawing of the sculpture or not Could it be free standing or have a base? I couldn't believe the enthusiasm as they left for their other classes.

As one of my extracurricular practices, I kept my camera in the closet and photographed the art projects in progress and the finished work that was placed in the Art

Wing showcase. It was emptied and ready when the students arrived with their pieces in brown paper grocery bags. I had not intended for it to be a competition but it was. The students who found making a found object sculpture difficult were spurred on by those who succeeded. I never inquired whether or how much input a parent made or where the material came from. That was the deal and I kept to it. Whatever the level of invention or success, each piece was accepted for the display case.

When I reported to them of the overwhelming praise their work had received, they insisted on telling their individual anecdotes about how they saw trash in a different light, overcame problems and finally the fear that something might happen to their work on the way to school from home. One child devised an elevator from a milk carton. Others created people from old toys and the cutest of animals. The Queen was voted the best. At the end of the presentation, I showed them that I too did the project. I called it, "Ballet". At term's end, I offered to return their work and many were happy to take theirs. Some insisted that I keep it to inspire future art students, which it did. I often wonder whether after forty years, if any of those children remember that art class or the profound satisfaction they gave me, and still do.

Forty years! That was a time, when as art coordinator, I was given a carte blanche and a catalogue full of materials to inspire creativity in young students, who were talented and eager. By a quirk of fate, I got the job as a temp, at a nearby Junior High replacing a teacher on sabbatical. There I remained for twenty years and have a collection of memories and souvenirs to show for it.

Crisis Management

After all the Ed courses and the manuals we read, there are unforeseen situations which arise in the classroom. The reaction to these by Junior High School students may vary but the chaos is probably universal and required emergency measures, even in the art class.

Although a 2 1/2-inch mouse scurrying across the floor created no menace to life or limb, the threat is not perceived that way. The girls began to scream and jump up on their chairs, bold

their skirts tightly around their legs and demand, "Get him! The boys charged out of their seats to track down the invader, each armed with an improvised weapon The poor beleaguered animal cowered in the corner of the room as I asked the class to calm down then got the broom and dustpan from the closet. It's only a little mouse!" I cautioned "Blam!" one of the boys has used his geography book to dispatch the creature to mouse heaven He did not wait

for the dustpan but picked up the mouse by the tail to taunt the horror stricken girls. He finally surrendered the body to the dustpan. Everyone was told to return to their seats and decorum was restored. Then, I seriously suggested that the class now has a subject to draw which brought comments of "Gross!" and "Yuck! My retort. Only kidding!" brought some laughter.

The heroic student was allowed to escort his victim, safely entombed in a manila envelope to the custodian's office. He soon returned to an ovation of applause and the lesson of the day proceeded as planned.

On occasion, purposeful acts of mischief were done to disrupt the normal classroom order. Soon after leaving the hallway, which I was ordered to supervise during passing, I entered the room to find the girls screaming. It was another time, another class and not a scurrying mouse but a filthy condom being kicked around the room by the boys. Upon my entrance, everyone scrambled to their assigned seats and assumed the appearance of complete innocence. I said nothing and took a sheet of construction paper to scoop it up and drop it into the trash basket next to my desk. Several students raised their hands to offer testimony as to whom the culprit was but I refused to recognize them. I merely said, "No need to have made a fuss! If you know what it was, no matter! If you don't know, no matter! It's garbage now! I ultimately found out which boy had started the prank but I wasn't going to let him succeed in stopping the lesson. Some time later, he had become a prize artist. He came to confess, privately and all I said was, "I know!"

Because I preferred to rearrange the desks in my room for different projects, they were not bolted to the floor. One Spring semester, I entered the room from hall duty and found several boys break-dancing in the back of the room. The desks had been shaved to the side to make room and the class plus some stray students were in a semi-circle clapping the rhythm beat I stood behind the crowd and un-noticed, watched the talented twists and somersaults being executed. Then someone noticed me and the children ran to their seats. Some rearranged the desks and chairs. Everyone expected a scolding! None came! In fact I said, "You guys are great! Only we can't create a situation where the Assistant Principal might get on my case."

So, I made a deal. "Let's not delay with the lesson and if we have time before the bell, we can move the furniture aside and have a few minutes of break-dancing." And so it was I had the lesson end ten minutes early and for several times we had the performance. Their enthusiasm often extended after the passing bell and I had to be stern with them to get them on their way. Because I had my prep period next, I volunteered to get the desks back in order, myself. When I sew the Gym teacher next and told him what happened, he arranged to include the break-dancing in his program, which made the use of the art room no longer necessary.

Graffiti on the walls in a school and elsewhere was frowned upon by the administration and custodial staff, obviously. One semester, I found a student in one of my classes with a bag full of marker pens. It was early in the term and I did not know the student at all. When I proceeded to questioned him he just closed down. The kid next to him spoke up and explained that his friend was a graffiti artist. "I asked, "Do you have anything to show me?" Without saying a word, he opened his book-bag where I beheld several books filled with the most intricate graffiti designs and lettering, as well as original comic strip figures. I had so many questions for him but that had to wait. Here was a prodigy that needed encouragement and support. The class went on with their daily assignment and he went on with his graphics. His individual style was unique. After the class. I got my answers and the pledge that none of his talent would end up on any walls inside or outside the building. I promised him that my deal included protecting him from the restrictions about carrying markers pens in school. I supplied him with as much drawing paper as he needed for his work in school and at home. I was able to scavenge cardboard cartons from appliances, left out for trash, so that he could enlarge his projects At the Spring festival that year, his large masterpiece in the lobby, brought praise from the audience and administration.

Over the course of time, it became apparent to me that there are talented art students and those that have difficulty. So, I decided to make templates of the figures for the less competent, giving them the option to participate according to their ability. The result was a successful and large collection of artworks at the end of the semester. One such display was the illustrations for Alex Haley's masterpiece, "ROOTS" which drew extraordinary praise, especially from the parents of the less talented students. My supervisor, at the end-term came to understand my logic although she had criticized it during her observation.

All too often, students would bring items to class which could be harmful or disruptive. I would try to deal with the issue by taking the object with the proviso that it would be returned after school or at the term's end. My idea was to prevent the pupil from getting into trouble and that I had no desire to punish them. In June, I had a collection of forgotten stuff at the beginning of my tenure, a science teacher complained, that one of my students spent time in his class, drawing nude figures in his books. I asked if they were anatomically correct. When he replied that they were, I said, "Encourage him!" At my retirement party, he told this story to the delight of the audience.

Extra-Curricular

In the course of my early teaching career, my involvement did not stop at the 8:00 to 3:00 time period or my room 212. My wife's union had an opportunity for members to go to Mexico the summer of '70 and we made plans to join them. The trip experience is related in a different piece, however, I wrote the Mexico City school system for a meeting with their Art Department. Their gracious reply was surpassed by the warm visit that following summer.

Being called "Professor" the word for teacher in Mexico was pleasing in itself but the fact that the four teachers took time away from their summer vacation les come to the Belle Artes Building for our get-together was even more gratifying. Fortunately, we had no problem conversing, although their English had some Spanish accent. (See Polaroid picture of smiles!)

They were very impressed with my reporting about the generous amount of funding we were received at that time, and the encouragement as well. Their explanation that only the talented children were given art classes was surprising to inc. When suggested having a reciprocal exchange of our middle school students' art work, they expressed eagerness. The resulting messages, which found accidently in a stack of letters om my personal file. It is this collection of record that has refreshed my memory of the wonderful change in Mexica of our art students work. The actual official messages have been copied as an evidentiary material.

Board of Education of the City of New York
COMMUNITY SCHOOL DISTRICT 29
221-10 Jamaica Avenue
Queens Village, N.Y. 11428

MAX G. RUBINSTEIN
Community Superintendent

FOR IMMEDIATE RELEASE

INTERNATIONAL ART EXHIBIT FEATURES WORK OF LINDEN JUNIOR HIGH SCHOOL

Max G. Rubinstein, Community Superintendent of District 29 in Queens announced that a collection of drawings and paintings by students of the Linden Junior High School, JHS 192 of District 29, were put on exhibit in the Exhibition Hall of the "Instituto Nacional De Bellas Artes" in Mexico City along with a similar exhibit from Japan, during the weeks of March 15, 1972 to April 10, 1972.

The selection of twenty pieces sent from the Art Department of the Linden Junior High School (JHS 192) located at 109-89 204th. Street, St. Albans, was very well received and gratitude was expressed in a letter from Professor Humberto Chavez Cabrales, Director of Artes Plasticas of the Mexican School System.

Mr. William Harris, Principal of Linden Junior High School, stated that the Art Exhibit was the culmination of many months of effort by Mr. Edward Miller, teacher of Art at the Linden Junior High School. This Exhibit was an outgrowth of a visit to Mexico City by Mr. Miller

A reciprocal Exhibit is being planned so that the students at JHS 192 can enjoy the works of the school children of Mexico.

Among the fine works presented for the Art Exhibit, outstanding contributions were made by the following students: Marchelle Grier, Gred Woods, Rickey Kelly, Martha Escobar, Edwain Garcia, and Christine Harvey.

INSTITUTO NACIONAL DE BELLAS ARTES

DE LA SECRETARIA DE EDUCACION PUBLICA
PALACIO DE BELLAS ARTES   MEXICO, D. F. - MEXICO

DEPARTAMENTO DE ARTES PLASTICAS
SECCION DE ENSEÑANZAS ARTISTICAS
OFICINA DE PROMOCION DE EXPOSI-
CIONES DE ARTE INFANTIL.

Oficio No. 285/72.

A 6 de marzo de 1972.
" Año de Juárez "

C. Profr. Edward Miller
168-44 127 TH Avenue,
Jamaica New York.
U. S. A.

    Con relación a su carta de fecha 17 de Octubre del año próximo pasado, girada a esta Sección de Enseñanzas Artísticas del Departamento de Artes Plásticas del I. N. B. A., tengo a bien informar a usted que hemos recibido lote conteniendo 20 Obras Artísticas de los Alumnos del "Linden Junior High School"

    Al mismo tiempo nos estamos permitiendo hacerle el envío de 41 Obras de niños mexicanos que asisten a Escuelas Primarias y Secundarias del Distrito Federal, México.

    Ruego a Ud. de la manera más atenta, si no tiene inconveniente alguno nos informe de la Difusión que le tenga preparada a este material, así como nos haga el envío de documentos gráficos.

    Anexamos al presente Invitación de la Exposición de Dibujo y Pintura "EXPRESION INFANTIL JAPONESA Y OBRAS DEL LINDEN JUNIOR HIGH SCHOOL 1922", que estará en exhibición en la propia Sala de Exposiciones de la Sección: sito, en Revillagigedo No. 22 México 1, D. F., del 15 de marzo al 10 de abril del presente.

    Agradeciendo de antemano las atenciones que otorgue al presente, me reitero a sus apreciables órdenes y quedo de usted como su Atto y S. S.

El Jefe de la Oficina
de Promoción de Exposiciones

ATENTAMENTE
EL JEFE DE LA SECCION

PROFR. HUMBERTO CHAVEZ CABRALES

Like The Bible

Strange as it may seem, one of my stories at Linden, JHS 192, reads like the bible, well not exactly. My time there began in 1967. In the beginning, Mr. Fox was the principal and the school was a happy place, as I and a staff of five art teachers started our tenure. It was integrated with white pupils bussed in from areas as Jamaica Estates and as far away as Floral Park, outside the surrounding black neighborhoods: Hollis, Jamaica and Cambria Heights.

The A.P., Mr. Abe Meyers, assigned to set up the teachers and pupils' programs. Proposed arranging the shop and specialty classes such as music, dance, art etc. joining two classes together, instead of four single ones and making 80 minute time period instead of separate 40-minute ones. This gave the teachers more time for classwork and less time to classroom logistics. The student body ran from 7th through the 9th grade, and the students' who chose the special art program, were allowed to express their enthusiasm and skills. Some of the other stories exemplify this, and my good fortune as a beginning teacher. Beginning September 1967.

Although Black History Month was yet to be declared, black history studies were offered in the Social Studies classes and integrating those lessons in the other disciplines was encouraged. So when it was offered in my special art classes and I rexographed material about the leaders in the Afro-American movement, the enthusiasm exploded. Each pupil was offered the choice of a hero or heroine to portray in pencil and finished with pastels. In addition to introducing each character, lessons were included about the anatomy of the head and portraiture. I was amazed by the artistry with which these students grasped the assignment. When the faces were completed, one of the pupils asked if he could include a related background as well. The rest of the class agreed and the idea was adopted enthusiastically.

When I explained the project to the assistant principal, she told it to Mr. Fox Soon he decided to visit my classroom and with his approval agreed that the portraits deserved a mural.

Before the work was complete, I found a discarded cardboard container from a delivered refrigerator and brought it to my room where it was prepared as a panel for the montage. After school, I coated it with acrylic paint and kept it in the storage room for it to dry. I used my "prep periods" to design the slogan piece and the title cards giving credit to each artist. The next lesson dealt with arranging each work. The girls insisted that Harriet Tubman and Sojourner Truth have prominece. The boys demanded Frederic Douglass and Booker T. be the ones. I suggested a committee be chosen and so when the layout was decided and I glued the pieces in place. The powdery chalklike pastel surface had to be scaled so I sprayed the whole thing with a clear acrylic.

With Dr. Fox's approval, Mr. Germains, the woodworking instructor, assembled a frame for the piece. I had one of the boys' volunteers to stay after school to paint the frame. It was hung on the right-hand wall in the lobby for everyone to see at the end-term concert where it received great praise. That was the last occasion for 192 to be an integrated school. The Genesis came to an end, became an Exodus! This happened during the early part of the new spring term. Warm outerwear was necessary in the winter weather. Suddenly, the seats of the white children in any room were empty. To my dismay, I learned that an expensive coat of one of the white boys was forcibly stolen. I had belonged to one of my prize pupils.

The mural hung for many years after Dr. Fox (cared his doctorate) had left his position. Many years it remained intact until it was defaced by some vandal. Despite the marking, it remained in place even after it was joined by Will Bush's "Civil Rights mural.

Dilemma

When I was assigned as a temp, covering for the art teacher on sabbatical, my supervisor, A.P., gave me two books: The Board of Education (archaic) Art Curriculum and Secondary School Art Projects. This was before classes started, so I looked through the material, carefully studying the suggestions. I was a mature adult, so I decided to put the books away on the top shelf of my coat closet. Instead, I adapted my college training instead, leaving them there until the day of my retirement, twenty years later when I returned them in perfect condition to a different A.P. in charge of the department.

That took care of the first dilemma, and there were more to follow. Some of my classes were made up of students who preferred the special art program and others were assigned art who had little or no interest in it. For those children, the attitude taught to them in the lower grades was, whatever you do in art class, a passing grade was assured. That art was not a major subject so they didn't have to do the work.

Another dilemma occurred during one of my early classes. It was taught to the children, that if they "Messed up!" another fresh paper would be given to them. This happened when a boy in my class began to wrinkle his paper and to tear it, demanding another sheet. I ordered him to stop "It's my paper!" he said. I stopped the classwork, to explain, "I gave the paper to you, I will collect it from you! Now let me see what you have done." I looked at the work, praising his achievement. I smother out the wrinkles and scotch taped the tears, making the deal. You will finish this paper, I'll then give you another, if you want it and give you the average grade. True to my word, I put the finished repaired paper in the drawer with the other classwork and he did it over without a flaw. Two things resulted... he became the star artist in that class and word managed to get to my other classes, and although they thought Mr. Miller was crazy, when it came to the mid-term and end-term shows, their collection was the best.

BOARD OF EDUCATION CITY OF NEW YORK
DISTRICT-29
LINDEN JUNIOR HIGH SCHOOL - 192Q
109-89 204 STREET
ST. ALBANS, N. Y. 11412
TEL. 479-5540

MR. WILLIAM N. HARRIS
PRINCIPAL

MR. J. TRAPANI
ADMINISTRATIVE ASSISTANT

RENEE SKLAR
WILLIAM EGGER
ABRAHAM MEYER
MONA ABAEL - SCIENCE
ABRAHAM RIFKIN - HEALTH ED.

January 10, 1972

Dear Mr. Miller:

I am writing to express my thanks and appreciation for your outstanding contribution to J.H.S. 192 during the Christmas Holiday Assemblies.

Your decorative art displays in the lobby and the auditorium enhanced the holiday atmosphere.

I look forward to the Spring Festical when we shall once again have a culminating Art Show for the pupils and the community to view.

Cordially yours,

Henrietta Berman
Assistant Principal

HB:BBM

WILLIAM H. HARRIS
principal

109-89 204th STREET
ST. ALBANS, N.Y. 11412

Board of Education...
City of New York...

Office Telephone
479-5540

Guidance Telephone
479-5547

ASSISTANTS TO PRINCIPAL

Mona Abel
Abraham Meyer
Frank Quiroga
Celestine Reid
Abraham Rifkin
Henrietta Rosner

June 25, 1973

Mr. Miller

Dear Mr. Miller:

    Once again, you've done an outstanding job in typing, layout and illustration of the school magazine, <u>Linden Liberator</u>.

    Despite short notice, you did an excellent job, as usual. My congratulations on the fine quality and overall fine work.

                             Yours truly,

                             A. Meyer
                             Assistant Principal

AM:AR

cc: Mr. Harris

Templates

Having classes of talented and motivated children is ideal, but when the office assigns other students to your program you are faced with a dilemma. One such class was of Special Ed. children who were obviously limited in their abilities. Another time, a class of recently arrived Haitian children, most of whom were only French speaking, was assigned to art in my room. At other times, individual problem students were put in my classes. I had to cope.

Teaching them art was not an option. Teaching them success was. I noticed that the woodworking instructor gave the students precut shapes, called templates, which were used to transfer a design onto the wood for processing. So, I decided to prepare templates made out of oaktag for these special classes. Although my supervisor frowned upon this 'easy way out, it proved to be a positive experience.

The movie "Jaws!" was playing in the theaters and when I gave out the template of a shark, the class was a buzz of excitement. After discussing the possibilities and showing my sample, the pupils were told they could trace one, two or more sharks and make their picture as scary as they wanted. Where I had pupils being mischievous throwing crayons, before, there was no nonsense now. After the lesson, each picture was displayed and an explanation was given about the choices that were made. It was surprising to see the different interpretation each child brought to the work.

Similarly, at another time, I prepared templates of the space-ship, "Voyager with the same instruction, giving each child the freedom of creating an interesting background. None of the papers ended up in the waste-paper basket. In fact, at the end-term concert, they were mounted and displayed in the school lobby. One of those children whose work was shown, introduced me to his mother after he had proudly shown her his drawing. His mother remarked that it was the first time any of his art was displayed. Subsequently, I decided to hang those drawings on the fence outside the school in a special art show, along with the art talent work, much to the neighborhood's approval.

By the end of my tenure, the amount of money for supplies was greatly reduced. Special projects were no longer available so others were instituted. Lessons in anatomy and perspective were given, as well as art slide shows that were available from the Board of Ed. library.

The number of art teachers had been reduced and I would have lost my job at Linden were it not for the more senior teacher deciding to take a leave, get married and have a baby. The fact is that a new principal took over, who felt the school would be better served with music and dance, may have had to do with it.

When the movie, "Roots" was showing in the theaters, almost every subject became connected to the theme. Most of the art projects were done on construction paper but I realized this one deserved something special. I had in my closet reams of newsprint, that is paper that newspapers are printed on, whose size is twice as large as construction paper. The talent classes went to work and the result was fantastic.

The only drawback was that the pictures of Kunte Kinte and Chicken George had to be done in crayon. Because of the thinness of the paper, special care had to be taken if erasure was necessary. The end result was beyond all expectation, especially when mounted and dis played. The principal made special mention of the art work at the Spring festival when the Africa motif was expressed in dance and drama. The lesser skilled students made their contribution with African masks, drawn with crayon on construction paper.

Of course, there were also exceptional projects all the time. In one of my classes, not talent, a student called to my attention his friend's secret. The boy kept a stash of markers in his book bag. When I asked to see what he was up to, he brought out five drawing pads with the most magnificent graffiti artwork I had ever seen.

Every page was completely covered with brilliantly covered action figures surrounded with three dimensional buildings and scenery. After thanking him and his friend for sharing this with me, I asked him to stay after class for a talk. Because, there was some graffiti vandalism going on, I cautioned the boy to continue keeping the pens hidden. I made a deal with him that instead of doing the regular class assignment, he could work on his special art. Whereas his book of drawings were 6x10 inches, he could now have drawing paper twice the size to draw on.

His contribution to the art show was a magnificent graffiti drawing six feet by twelve feet.

One morning on the way to work, I saw a discarded cardboard box by the side of the road. It had contained a new refrigerator and I immediately visualized it as a perfect project for my graffiti artist. Well, perfect wasn't an exaggeration, according to the reaction of the audience who saw it on display in the school lobby. The caricatures of the principal and teachers that he included in that work was astounding.

I was very fortunate to have the occasional genius come into my life. In another non-talent class. I was again tipped off about a student with exceptional ability. He was not timid about his skill and when he brought an envelope to class, I was puzzled. He said that he wanted to do the logo in the return address which was a beautiful tiger. What was special about the picture was that it was made up of black stripes on the white background, no color, no outline. I had to bring him a sheet of heavy paper from my own supply, 18 x24".

The original picture was no bigger than one inch from which he copied the enlarged figure. Amazing! He did it all by eye, using no grid or other technique artist's use. In addition to using India ink, he used shades of gray. When I explained what "Trompe l'oeil" meant, he was very pleased. It is a French phrase meaning, 'trick the eye'. What is left out is filled in by the brain, so no outline of the tiger was needed to be drawn. At the end of the term, he graduated and his graduation present was that magnificent tiger, for me Marie and Michele were in my talent class several terms, they were identical twins and they often switched seats to trick me. They were excellent artists and a joy to have in my class.

Of all the graduating students I had the pleasure of teaching, they were the only ones who gave me their yearbook photos. Those beautiful faces are still laughing at me.

Sample Of Creativity Using Templates

Mr. Miller's Outdoor Exhibit in May

BOARD OF EDUCATION OF THE CITY OF NEW YORK

JHS 192	Queens	11412	109-89 204 St.	479-5540
SCHOOL	BOROUGH	ZIP CODE	ADDRESS	TELEPHONE

OFFICE OF THE PRINCIPAL

May 25, 1984

Mr. Edward Miller

Dear Mr. Miller:

In behalf of the pupils, parents, administration and members of the community, I wish to commend you for the outstanding street fair art exhibit held last Thursday evening during our Gala Spring Festival of Music and Art.

This exhibit which you affixed to the wire fence showed off the art talent of our pupils and it attracted hundreds of visitors from the community who commented favorably on this innovation of our school.

I also wish to express my appreciation for the program cover contest which you conducted and for your expertise in photographing the evening concert.

Your continued dedication to this school is over and above the call of duty.

principal

109-89 204th STREET
ST. ALBANS, N.Y. 11412

City of New York

Office Telephone:
479-5540

Guidance Telephone
479-5547

ASSISTANTS TO PRINCIPAL

Mona Abel
Abraham Meyer
Frank Quiroga
Celestine Reid
Abraham Rifkin
Henrietta Rosner

June 19, 1973

Mr. Edward Miller

Dear Mr. Miller:

Before the year vanishes, I should like to thank you "for the record" for your many contributions above and beyond the call:

1. Your thoroughness as Art Chairman in exhibits and supplies

2. The attractive and worthwile mural produced by your Major Art Class which is now in a permanent disply in our lobby

3. Your assistance in your second floor hall assignment and at dismissal time

4. Your dedication in photographing the Spring Music Assembly, as well as other important events which leaves us with a permanent movie film collection of these activities.

Sincerely yours,

Henrietta Rosner
Assistant Principal

HR:BBM
cc:file
    Mr. Harris

30

The Bureau

No! It wasn't the FBI! It was the Board of Education; Bureau of Supplies and it was one of the wonders in my life. The position of art teacher that I was assigned to, came as a last resort. Except for the regular art teacher at Linden Junior High School opting to take her sabbatical at that very time, there would have been no opening for me and no beginning job.

Linden was a new school in St Albans, Queens, not far from the new co-op apartment that I and my family had just occupied. The staff were newly assigned as was the Principal, so there was not an old clique to contend with. Also, my good fortune came with an Assistant Principal who was a weekend painter, and much attuned to an Art Department's needs.

So, one day, when Mr. Gaston came to my room and handed me a thousand-page book from the Bureau of Supplies and told me, as art coordinator to select items for the department, I was literally in shock. He calmly explained that he had gotten $1200 of the school's funding for books and art supplies and he needed me to make a list of purchases This was Nirvana, the year of 1971.

When he left, I looked through the art pages and found much more than crayons. There was an opportunity to fill the art storeroom with goodies far beyond my dreams. I consulted with the other art teachers and received little advice. All they wanted was paper stock for drawing, painting and pastels. They had no idea what wealth of material was available. The first year. I was timid in my selection but with the experience of having students who were talented, cooperative and smart, I subsequently improved up on my shopping list.

Included materials to decorate the Superintendent's office for its annual art exhibit. This connection had me visit the other district schools teaching the teachers how to display the art work done in their classes. Holiday decor was an important area of interest which I was volved in, in addition to my own school responsibilities

One year, I thought to teach art printing, what I learned in college as engraving. In the print shop, the material to be printed is already prepared but in the art class the process of printing is the last step and everything is done by hand. In lieu of copper plate, used by great masters like, Rembrandt, I was able to order blocks of linoleum, gouging tools, brayers, printers' ink and rollers, all part of the project. Were it not for the fact that the students were cooperative and responsible, the effort would have failed.

The winter holiday was a month away, so the idea of designing Christmas cards seemed to be an exciting thing to teach. Again, the tools were hazardous if used carelessly, so required parental permission. Much time and patience was necessary before the actual work began unlike ordinary drawing, the image created had to be cut in reverse, so that the negative would produce a positive when printed.

The students were duly impressed to learn that I had worked in printing long before I returned to college to become a teacher. This practical knowledge helped the students appreciate my instructions more fully. My 8th graders made Xmas cards, on smaller blocks, while the 9th graders had the option of using the larger size linoleum to engrave winter scenes.

The principle that the engraving must be the reverse of their actual drawing was the one obstacle to overcome. This was a project that caught the imagination of the children, and I was amazed at the energy they invested. The use of the cutters required utter concentration and care. Because the cuttings needed to be thrown away, each table captain saw to it that the trash was confined and disposed of at the end of each session.

If words were included, they had to be cut backwards as the pupil's initials were. One particular story remains vividly in my mind Whereas most children in the class opted to cut a symbolic card, such as a tree, wreath candies or stockings, he decided to cut a fireplace with several stockings hanging down from the lintel. Every so often, I would check on his progress, and was pleased with the work. Near the end, he stopped me from seeing it, and I assumed that he wanted to surprise me. And so he did.

He applied the ink appropriately and made the first impression. The shout that came from him, I'll never forget. "Oh! No!" I rushed over to his table as he began to tear up the print I was able to stop him and saw that the beautiful fireplace and stockings were perfectly rendered. The surprise he hid from me were the words, "MERRY XMAS" cut into the top of the fireplace, only it read backwards. In his haste he had forgotten to reverse the letters. The poor kid was devastated. I ruined it! I ruined it!" he kept crying. He wouldn't let me put my arms around him. I told him that there's a solution. Not as terrific as his original idea, but almost.

"Why not just cut away the area with the letters. I suggested "Then the fireplace will have a white marble front piece, and no-one would ever know what happened. Just be careful not to accidentally spoil the rest of the work! That will be our secret! And so it was. His print of the fireplace with stockings was so wonderful that I encouraged him to make up a dozen cards. I provided him with envelopes so he could give them to his other teachers, the principal and friends. His work and the others became part of the holiday showcase display.

Keith Waite
8-Major-Art

Debra James
8 Major Art

Student Teacher

The second week in September, my assistant principal called me into his office. I had just been assigned to IHS 192 Queens, as a permanent substitute art teacher and Mr. Gaston my supervisor, assured me that as a beginner, I was going to get all the help necessary to successfully carry out my duties. Two months into the term, he asked me to see him again. I tried not to show my fear as I waited to be signaled into his office and beckoned to sit.

"Mr. Miller," he began. "I've been watching you for these several weeks..." My heart began to sink. "...and the principal and I have determined that you..." My heart sank deeper! "That you will be able to have a student teacher in your class."

I was too shocked to speak for several minutes. I had assumed that something bad was going to happen. Instead, I was being given the responsibility of helping train another art teacher.

I could not decide whether I should remind him that I had begun my own teaching career just five weeks before, so I said nothing. The telephone rang and he excused himself while he talked to the caller. This gave the knots in my stomach time to unravel and I breathed easier. His call ended and he turned to face me.

"I would have hesitated giving this job to you but of all the art teachers, you are the most mature. I observed you in the room and from the hallway and I am confident that you can handle this well." When supervisors officially observe a lesson, they must prepare a written report and discuss it with the teacher. I had no idea that he was observing me unofficially. "You've just come through it yourself, so you are well equipped for the job. Besides, I am right next door, if you need help. The young lady,

Miss Trabel, will start next Monday and we'll give her the best art class of the seventh grade. You have the weekend to think it over. I trust you will do it!" He stood and I stood. We shook hands and I returned to my classroom, much bewildered by the prospect that lay before me, the extra responsibility in addition to my own teaching schedule.

Monday came and Mr. Gaston escorted the Queens College student into my room. The class was busy with their assignment and I continued checking their work. Both the A.P. and student teacher took seats in the back of the room. I found one piece of work that was extremely well done and I held it up to the class, indicating its merit. When I asked if anyone needed help, several hands were raised. I stopped at the desk of those children who indicated their need for special attention and helped resolve their problem. Shortly before the bell rang, the work was collected and the next project was suggested. I kept the papers on my desk after the students left for their next class in order to show my future charge a sample of the lesson. When we finished, Mr. Gaston handed a drawing that he had done at the time he was in the back of the room. We all had a laugh when instead of just approving it, I suggested a correction in the perspective.

Miss Trabel and Mr. Gaston were able to see the work product of the class she was going to teach When the Art Supervisor left, I introduced myself further and gave her an understanding of what lay ahead of us. I had rexographed several copies of my lesson plans and gave her some empty forms for her to write up. She met with this class twice a week and after sitting in for a month, we decided she was ready to take over. The students were beautiful and received her with the same attention and courtesy as they had me. She loved teaching art and it showed in her presentation and success. Whatever needed sharpening was discussed in office hours, during my prep period, which immediately followed the class session. One day she asked why I had the students drawing a frame around their papers with one inch wide cardboard strips.

She was surprised by my reply.

"It was customary for students to write their name, class and seat number on the back of the paper." I explained "Drawing a frame served several purposes: it had them print their name, class and seat number along the bottom edge for immediate identification, even as the work was in progress and made distribution simple. It acted as a barrier that prevented getting the desk dirty from painting over the edge of the paper and it also added a professional look to the finished work. The few minutes it took to draw the frame was well worth the trouble."

She agreed with the wisdom of my method. "We'll call it the Miller system!" she offered.

Then I confessed my real reason. Having over two hundred different children in my art classes made remembering all their names impossible. With the information right in front, it was easy to know each student's name. The college had prepared her well and her lesson plans were flawless. She greatly appreciated sharing my own student teaching experiences with her as well as the write up that I had to prepare. The drawing lessons were the "Still-Life" based on the work of the artist Cezanne. My supply of wax fruit and vegetables set up as models, gave inspiration. Her enthusiasm and knowledge inspired the children and they produced fine results.

Mr. Gaston kept a vigilant eye on us both, gave us complete support and reported our progress to the principal. Her college professor paid us a surprise visits and found us prepared. When the holiday program needed the artwork, her class was honored with a special display. She stayed over her required time to assist in mounting the artwork on large construction paper for hanging around the school When the evening of the concert came. She received recognition along with the art staff, for a job well done from the Master-of-ceremonies.

It was then that she reported her not returning for the Spring term.

"I guess you know, I passed!!" she laughed. "I can't thank you enough. Mr. Miller."

"Susan, call me Ed! I would love to hear from you when you get your license! We'll have to celebrate! Isaid.

It was shortly after my retirement that I met Ms. Trabel accidentally at the art museum in Roslyn. She had been teaching on the North Shore of Long Island and bed since become a district art supervisor. We celebrated over a long overdue cup of coffee, reminisced about 192 and wished each other well. We exchanged addresses and when Christmas holiday arrived, I sent her a photograph of a "Still-Life drawing from the class she taught over twenty years before.

The Observation

In the course of my acting as mentor to the young lady, future teacher, I had to prepare her for the surprise observations that she would get from her college professor. When she had become comfortable with my coaching, I thought she would appreciate hearing about a special experience that happened to me only a short time ago. It was at my final observation in the Junior High School in Harlem and it shows the need to be flexible when following one's lesson plan.

The rule of the C.C.N.Y. School of Education that required student-teachers to be observed four times a semester. Mr. Bromwell, my mentor gave me more opportunities to work than most teachers do because at that time I was a mature adult. The school was very old in fact a new modern IS139M was being built along the East River, further north in Harlem. The class that I worked with was the 7 S.P., a group of well-mannered smart children with whom I immediately connected. Very often, when I was in charge. Mr. Bromwell would disappear, leaving the whole responsibility in my hands His confidence in my training paid off for this day I was to be observed by my college professor as well as the school principal, Mr. Giordano.

I had prepared my visual aids and supplies for each child. Each student had a rexograph booklet with explanations and homework assignment. They also had drawing paper, a T-square and sharpened #2 pencil. I even set the materials on the observers' desks. My introductory remarks dealt with the way the medium of drawing and painting depended on the skills of observation. I had some students help demonstrate the principles of perspective and point of view. When I asked for questions, there were very good points raised by the class. To demonstrate the example of blocking. I used the smallest boy and the biggest boy, much to the amusement of the whole class. This lead to the subject of "Point of View".

I planned to have the students look out the window from their seats, then do the same thing, standing. The change in elevation would show a different view. As I was about to tell the class to rise, I observed a group of men and a girl having sex on the rooftop across the street.

From the sitting position they could not see the rooftop, but standing, there would be mayhem. I suggested that we might better make the experiment in the glass room. The observers did not understand the change in plan when I had the top of my desk show the different perspective when sitting and standing, nor did I ever explain the change.

I lead the class in an exercise in linear perspective and the drawings were successfully executed. As I passed around the room, I checked the drawings and was happy to observe that Mr. Bromwell, my professor, and the principal had all followed my instructions to a "T". Two minutes before the bell rang, the drawings and materials were collected. The world was saved to be included in the reports. Needless to say the observation was successful and the day after my C.C.N.Y. graduation, Mr. Giordano, the principal, put me to work will the cad of the team. He even invited me to come work in the fall.

The big smile on her face said how much the story incent to her.

Student as Model… Mr. Miller's 7th Grade Art Class

Ed Miller's Video Class c.1980

Because Mr. Miller was given a substantial Art Department budget, he was able to give his SP class video lessons which involved script writing and acting as well as video photography on primitive equipment. The proficient students photographed special assembly programs for the school's archives.

"1st remove the lens cap!"

Hallway Crises

My art room 212, was at the wing's intersection with the Chemistry Department, so there was a lot of traffic during passing. The A.P., Ms. Berman/Rosner was adamant about my being on hall duty, even though it was a hardship for me getting my material ready for the incoming class. Sometimes I had the good fortune of volunteers who took the attendance or distributed the paper to their rightful desk.

But it was the hallway that was in crisis. During passing one day, a mob of students collected outside my room, surrounding a fight between two 9th grade girls. I made my way through the crowd telling them to get to their class and squeezed in between the two belligerents, daring them to hit me. Being two of my students, they pulled back and went into my classroom to their seats, fortunately, far apart.

The crowd had dispersed, the hall cleared and I entered my room. Everyone had taken their seats as I got their attention. I'm glad your fight was not in my room!" I said, trying to sound serious. "Was some boy worth losing a clump of hair, over?" I had kicked the wad of hair removed from one of the girl's head to the side from the center of the hall where it had fallen.

"It wasn't a boy!" one of the girls argued. "She said…" "No, I didn't!" protested the other, rising from her seat. I quickly move to stop her from moving anywhere. Actually, it was a third girl who had started the rumor that caused, the row. All this over nothing. Well, to the offended teenager "it wasn't nothing." Later in the term, the two hallway combatants became the best of friends.

We had frequent fire drills at Linden, but we never had a real fire in all my time, except one. As I mentioned before, the chemistry rooms were not far from the art wing. The one closest mine was vacant this one hot June day. Some student, taking advantage of that and that the door was left open, took advantage and set fire to the books in the bookcase located close to the door. I was finishing up the lesson when the fire alarm gong rang its signal.

Not realizing that it was not just a drill, I had the students leave their work on the desk, pick up their books, line up and walk 'not run' toward the required exit. When I opened the door a blast of smoke hit me, so I ordered the students to rapidly walk in the exit direction, not to look for the fire. When some boys did, I had to chase them away from the chemistry room. There were no other teachers at that place as students came running from the other part of the floor past the smoke, some to look for it, some to escape.

As one girl was running past the door, a boy pushed her into the room, where she gulped in a mouthful of the smoke, gasping and almost collapsing to the floor. Fortunately, I saw what had happened and was able to catch her before she fell. Instinctively, I threw her over my shoulder, like I'd seen firemen do, and ran down the hallway, hollering to let me pass, entering the stairwell and managing to reach the outer doorway into the fresh air.

I carefully set her down on the sidewalk, holding her up while telling her to breath. Her strength returned as I heard a woman neighbor across the street, who had seen us, beckon for me to bring the girl over to her house. She kindly took her in, took the time to help the girl recover. Where I had gotten the strength, I don't know. I then sought out my students who had assembled on Hollis Ave. as taught in the drills.

During all this time, the fire department had arrived and quenched the bookcase fire.

The smoke lingered on despite having all the windows fully opened. Where the A.P. was during all this, I have no idea. I'm sure none of this story can be verified, except by the author.

A Special Deal

The year was 1969, and my memory of this student was non-existent or close to it. I remember his name, Al Carrion, and his class, 9-15 because of his contribution to the yearbook, which triggered my memory. Dr. Fox was still the principal of 192 and it was still integrated.

Our first encounter occurred when I distributed paper and pencils in the select art class and he asked to be excused. He claimed that the classroom was not conducive to his creativity, me something in confidence, what the atmosphere was, that made me understand. When he showed me the two masterpieces, it made my decision clear.

The portrait of the Beetles' John Lennon, in India Ink wash on 14"x17" watercolor paper and a portrait of John the Baptist, also in India Ink offer a blue wash background, 10x14". I understood the secret. After the rest of the class proceeded with the classwork, I explained what our deal had to be.

In addition to doing the class art assignment at home, he could not sit idly in class. He could work on other class assignments or homework. I gladly gave him paper and art supplies which he tried to decline. The class held the secret in confidence. Our deal proved successful as he fulfilled our agreement and then some. His work was fantastic.

The supervisor was pleased with the work, unaware of the deal. When the end of the term came near and the yearbook was being formed, I suggested he do a portrait of Dr. King.

It arrived the next class, over the weekend. He had evolved into a new genre, pen and ink drawing… So proficient was his skill, that I had him design the cover. In addition he offered other drawings. His request for additional copies was the least reward for my graduate art genius!

Long after Al's graduation, I told my art teacher associate. Harold Gadsen, the story. He couldn't believe it. When he saw the yearbook and the two portraits, he agreed that he would have made the same deal, without regret!

REV. DR. MARTIN LUTHER KING, JR.
1929 - 1968

Linden J.H.S. Graduates

Linden Leaves 1969

Edward Miller 1G
16844 127th Ave.
Jamaica, N.Y. 11434
1-718-276-1507

Jan. 15. 2015

Dear Mr. Al Carrion, Artist

In my 89th year, I am attempting to create a memoir with pictures of my carreer as art teacher in IS192Q, the Linden School in St. Albans, Queens. I had a brilliant artist student who graduated in 1969, who produced great work for the yearbook and gave me a treasure of work which will be included in the book. If you are that person, please contact me asap as it will give me great pleasure and make up for the years that have passed. Tried to reach you on the computer through Linkedin but need your e-address. Called your phone, got a reply message from "David." BTW... If you are not the Al Carrion, my former student, help me find him, please.

sincerely,

ED Miller

Ed Miller, Art Teacher, Ret.
eedml257@aol.com

CAMPBELL, STEPHEN 9-5
Stock Room, Dean Monitor, Music

CARNEVALE, JOSEPH 9-8

CARRION, ALFRED 9-15

Teacher Teacher!

Teaching children in grades 6 through 9, was what I was faced with as I began work at 192Q. Subsequently, the grade 6 was eliminated and restored to Elementary school. Forty years later, the memories have become vague but thanks to my collection of photographs and a number of triggers, the stories return.

When Mrs. Rosner became my A.P., she took an attitude toward me that was often mean spirited. Some said that it was because of our comparable ages, my being two years older.

That she had come from an Elementary school setting, where the teachers were dependent on her for every decision and here we were relatively independent. It might have been my ides to have frames drawn as a border on each paper with the student's name, class and seat number printed on the front, violated her Elementary school system. My method also prevented leeching paint etc. onto the desk. The other factor was her authority issue.

The stock room, where I had control of supplies and used for storage of my special projects became an issue when she decided to adopt it for her personal closet Being my boss made it a no issue situation for me, but it was for her. She was unhappy that the Principal spoke in my favor regarding its usage. One day, however, it proved a godsend. Without informing me, she had placed a stack of Sanitary Napkins on a shelf near the outer door. The inner door connected to my art room. One day, a girl in my art class raised her hand, Teacher! Teacher!", she cried out Mary is having her…! too embarrassed to continue. Suddenly the class became chaos, I told Mary and her friend to come with me toward the closet room, where I opened the door for her, told her to take the box that she needed and attend to the problem. Closing the door, I told her to knock when she was ready. As she reamed to her seat, I informed the class that I had a 10 year old daughter in Andrea Jackson High School, not to be embarrassed

Shortly afterward, in another class, another student interrupted the lesson with the same issue. It then occurred to me that there was a need for additional safety pins, so I kept a few in my wallet, just in case. Why the girls came to me instead of the Health Ed teacher or Mrs. Rosner, I can't understand. I wonder if the girls could see the smile in my eyes.

One day, a young boy was brought to my classroom. I was not told anything about him, that it was his first day in an American school, that he was from the Islands, Bahamas. When the other boys snickered at the sight of his short pants and tie, I had to interrupt the lesson to talk about tolerance and acceptance. His name was Victor, but I never said it, so as not to encourage further disruption.

I gave him the materials and minimal instruction, suggesting he observe what the other children were about. Happily he created no problem until he raised his hand and meekly, called out, "Teacher, sir!" When I came over to him, he whispered that he needed to use the toilet I wrote out a pass and directed him to the boy's lavatory. A moment after he left, he returned, too soon to have resolved the problem. He beckoned to me to bend down to hear him whisper, "There are no doors!" It was a good thing that only I heard him because it would be cause for an uproar and teasing him, forever.

Fortunately it was close to the passing bell so I asked him to hold it. My lunch period followed, so I took Victor down to the teacher's men's room and stood guard until he finished.

As he exited, a fellow teacher saw what happened and chastised me for doing such a thing I was happy that Victor went on to his next class, where I hoped that teacher would have a better solution Actually, I never saw him again but be left me with a story never forgotten I was brought up in the era of ultimate respect for teacher. So, when faced with the attitude of Mrs. Rosner toward me, I was dismayed. Maybe it was my fault. The other art teachers became socially friendly with her, as with the other supervisors, I did not. Two incidents plague me to this day. Because my room 212, was adjacent to her office, she decided to use it for her A.P. meetings. The truth is that only my art room war kept clean and orderly. Because other departmental teachers were under her supervision, there were many other teachers present. Most of the discussion did not relate to me or my work, I decided to finish what I was doing, coming five minutes late.

Upon my arrival, she spent five minutes berating me with a tirade reserved for some criminal behavior. So intimidating was she that no one said a word. Even my excuse was ignored. When her face returned to the normal white, she got back to her talk. Suddenly, Ms. Frasier, the sweet, black music teacher opened the door and slid into a nearby chair. The A.P. turned to the teacher and said, "Miss Frasier! I would appreciate all the teachers arrive promptly to these meetings!" CASE CLOSED!

It seems that the other teachers attending these meetings in my room apparently had no respect or regard for others. I always took care to keep my room orderly, so when I returned after one of her meetings to find all the desks and chairs in disarray, I asked her to please ask the visitors to return my room to its original condition. Her response was a curt, "IT IS NOT YOUR ROOM! Enough said.

At my retirement party, when all the staff gave me a warm send off, she approached me to wish me well I refused to shake her extended hand and when she said, "I was a real bitch I replied, "Yes you were!" and walked away.

An earlier Assistant Principal, Mr. Egger, had a different point of view. It was mandatory to visit the classroom unannounced for an observation. The weekly lesson plans had to be prompt and carefully adhered to regardless of any change in circumstances. For some reason, his visit was expected, and the class visited was one that had the superior students. If it made the teacher look good, it made the supervisor look better. After each of these sessions, a copy of the observation report was given to the teacher for "Approval" and signature, to be placed in the teacher's file.

Mr. Egger's analysis of the lesson was exceptional. His report on the class participation, flawless. The summation and product achieved, super. The one flew was clear. "The window shades were uneven!" What could I do but agree and sign it. The next term, he observed my class. I made sure that the window shades were perfectly aligned. Oddly enough, most classrooms window shades were in disrepair, not mine. When the report came for my approval, we were given the opportunity to reject the findings, I was elated. A perfect score, almost. A small wad of paper was found in the corner of the room, noted and reported. According to Mrs. Rosner, if 'it was not my room', why was I responsible for that piece of paper?

Seldom did the head-custodian, Mr. Readous clean in the art wing but the woman, Mrs. Nurse, who usually did it, was out ill. One afternoon, Mr. Bill Readous, was finishing up in 'My" room, when I returned. We were on friendly terms, so I was surprised when he asked me, apologetically, "Mr. Miller, don't you teach in your classes?" I laughed and asked why, so he remarked that all the other art classrooms are littered with paper, a real mess. "Not yours!"

I led Bill over to the huge cabinet in the middle of the room where I slid open several of the drawers whose class numbers were tagged in the slot. "Here are all the papers done by the children. Everyone saved for the Parent-Teacher's conference and later to be put on display at the Christmas and Spring festivals." I continued, "Do you have a minute?" Then I explained.

"I always wait for the opportunity, to lose my cool when a student decided to destroy his Work, crumpling it, declaring, "I messed up!" I would stop him, take his paper, straighten it out and mend it with Scotch tape, if it had gotten torn. "It is my paper!" the child would protest "Wrong! I would counter. "Who gave you the paper?" No response. Then the sermon!

"If you "Mess up!" it is only your opinion. Maybe you didn't or maybe it could be fixed. You don't get another paper to mess up before I see that you finished the first one. In my class, the object is to create work not destroy work." I then place the mended paper back on his desk.

The whole class got the message and from then on no 'Messing up!' including that kid, who became a top student".

Bill shook my hand and left the room laughing, as never saw before. He became a pal.

| JHS 192 | Queens 11412 | 109-89 204th Street | 479-5540 |

November 15, 1982

Mr. Edward Miller

Dear Mr. Miller:

I would like to acknowledge, for the record, the quality of your lesson plans submitted so far this term. Your lesson goals are worthwhile, and on the appropriate level of your pupils. These goals are followed by stimulating motivations, pivotal questions and/or step by step development as well as summaries and a relevant homework assignment. Your plans are numbered and the top sheet enables me to determine what you are teaching every period.

I trust that you will continue these high professional standards throughout the school year.

Sincerely yours,

HENRIETTA ROSNER
Assistant Principal

Noted: _____
MARTIN DREW, Principal

ra

cc: Teacher's file
Art Department Meeting
Ann DiPiola, Ed Miller, Lucie Alcock
Ms. Rosner, A.P.

Crayons, Crisis, Creativity

For the classes that had two periods together, it was possible to have the children use that were more difficult to handle. For the one period classes, simpler coloring material more prudent, such as crayons. I distributed boxes of Crayola crayons to each child with the advice that they are responsible to return the remaining crayons in the box at class end. Of course it was expected that crayons may break, so the pieces would also go into the box. Mostly these conditions were adhered to except for the errant student who decided to break one on purpose to throw it at another student. When this happened, a strong warning was given that the crayons would not be given to the class. If the child was apprehended, his job was to find and collect all the pieces off the floor and not be given them again. All the others did fabulous work.

Another Crisis

Entering from hall duty one day, I found two boys playing a very dangerous game. They obviously did not realize just how dangerous their actions were. One student would take a defensive pose, as the other pulled back to affect the hardest blow into his partner's chest. The blow into the heart caused a momentary blackout/buzz. The harder the blow, the greater the sensation.

Of course when they saw me, they took their seats. What followed was a lecture, not about art but about death. Had they known of the dangerous consequences, they confessed, they would not have played this dangerous game. I explained, it would be terrible to lose my best artists.

Mr. Tag Along

It was at I.S.192Q that special events, visiting dignitaries and the many unique programs such as the Christmas show and the end term program, required keeping a photographic record.

The annual school yearbook needed an adept staff member, one who could be relied upon at a moment's notice to get the right shot. Who else but Mr. Miller, the art teacher, who kept his 35mm Nikon camera, loaded with film in his coat locker... More than half of the book had the pictures of the graduates and the other of the staff and activities. One year, the Parents' Association arranged for a professional crew to take the senior pictures, including the various sports teams One day, after the official photos came back, Mr. Miller was summoned to the principal's office "We have an emergency! We have to reshoot the basketball team picture!" So he grabbed his camera and took the team shot again. When he saw the original picture, he realized what the problem was. The team captain, holding the basketball, had kneeled in the middle of the group, in his shorts, without a jock-strap!

When the school superintendent, or some dignitary came to speak at an assembly program, or any special holiday assembly was planned, Mr. Miller was there to shoot the show. If the assistant to the Principal didn't think of it, Mr. Miller certainly did. Arrangements were quickly made to cover his class and he did himself proud. The school was graced by the performance of the "Wizards, a Harlem Globetrotters copy. If timing was key to the tricks they did, then it was great timing that got Mr. Miller to the basketball court in time to shoot the show.

Because his program schedule gave him a study period or administrative duty the last period of the day, he was permitted to leave early on "school" business, sometimes to have the film processed, so the pictures would be ready to show the next day. This impressed the Principal and staff immensely. Amassing a vast collection of photographs over the year made it possible for Mr. Gadson, the graphic arts teacher to make the senior magazine a masterpiece each year.

Because he was not actually a homeroom teacher, especially for a senior class, Mr. Miller was not supposed to be involved in the perks. However, by ingratiating himself to the administration in many ways, the exception was made. In addition to the senior teachers, parent volunteers made up the necessary number of escorts required on each school bus trip to ensure safety and supervision. Mr. Miller would tag along with his camera.

Each year, a committee of seniors would choose a trip destination and plans would be made, money collected. One year the children opted to visit the Franklin Institute of Science

in Philadelphia. That trip was unusual because usually the students opted for fun at Rye Beach in upstate New York. It was easier to shoot the kids having a blast, calling Mr. Miller to take their picture on the rides or posed. On one such trip he was enlisted to search the Playland grounds for two girls who turned up missing at roll call, before returning home. Riding home in the Principal's car may have been great, except for the worry that something amiss had happened. The next day, it was cleared up when the girls confessed to leaving without telling that a relative had come to take them home.

Because he was accustomed to escort extra-curricular activities, when the senior class prepared to attend the "Nutcracker!" at the New York City Ballet one Christmas, he was invited to join them by one of the music teachers. Seeing it on the television cannot compare with sitting in the last row in the balcony of the theater.

Mr. Miller's collaboration on the yearbook every year, was a labor of love Mr. Gadson and he spent many hours arranging the pictures and captions. Many of the photos that were used or discarded remain in his special file. The home library, has a twenty-year collection of Linden School yearbooks, a sampling of tag-along photography, a treasure trove of memories

The occasion is rare when a teacher receives a message that his class is covered for some emergency but I have some. One morning, returning after a special duty at the 29th District Office. I was leaving my car on the street near 192, when a truant student ambled by, waved to me, but did nor enter the school. It was close to the end of the second period and I made haste to meet my third period class.

Shortly into the lesson, I received a message that I was covered, and to go down to the principal's office. All kinds of terrible images passed through my mind, none happy, so when Mr. Harris told me that my car had been vandalized, I was relieved, that the driver's side window was smashed. It was not until years later that my suspicion made sense.

It occurred to me that whoever reported the crime, had to know it was Mr. Miller's car, and that boy had to be the one Fortunately, the principal had allowed me to take the car and get the repair done before returning to work. Luckily, my insurance covered glass repair, cost free.

On open school night, I took pictures of visiting parents and teachers, just in case the editor of "The Linden Legend", our school newspaper would need them. It became expected for photos to be shot whenever dignitaries and officials came to grace a special assembly program, so arrangements were made to cover my classes. Fortunately, the students were accustomed to carry on with their work while I was away and gave no trouble.

When it was suggested that I join the senior day trip to Washington, D.C., it was a big surprise but not as big as with the kids waiting to ascend the Washington Monument. Standing patiently below its women's voice called out from a distance. A young lady dressed in a National Parks Department (Smokey the Bear, hat and all.) uniform came marching toward me, gave me a hug and a kiss, to my surprise and everyone else on the line.

She was a student Morehouse College and was working parttime for the service and was a former student of mine at Linden, their school, many years before. She updated me on her life and I on mine. We saluted each other as she left on the rounds and we entered the obelisk and the elevator to the top. The students were amazed as I was.

VOL. VI, No. 2 LINDEN JUNIOR HIGH SCHOOL, ST. ALBANS April 1969

Feature Teacher
MRS. WINSTON

Mrs. Winston is not only a sewing teacher but a housewife as well.

Her talent, of course, helps her to be a good housewife. She makes clothes for herself and her family. Sewing is important to everyone, says Mrs. Winston. The girls will find out in their older years, that the knowledge of some kind of sewing will be very useful.

Mrs. Winston became a Home Eco. teacher because she thought it to be a most interesting field. When Mrs. Winston was a young girl she liked to share the everyday chores such as cleaning the house and helping her mother cook and sew. As a result she became a Home Eco. teacher in the field of Sewing.

She has been a Sewing teacher now for several years.

Mrs. Winston's family including her older daughter and son are also in the teaching field. She also has a young son who keeps her posted on the teen scene of today.

Toni Lipscomb

```
FEATURE TEACHER
NEXT ISSUE:
MR. MELORE
```

Linden Basketball Team Wins Queens Title

Art For The Yearbook

Mr. Miller, Art Coordinator for the school, has been art adviser for the yearbook for the past two years. Last year the book won second place in the Columbia Scholastic Press Association Contest.

The art work is based on the poems and stories the literary committee, headed by Mrs. Jackson, produces for the yearbook. The theme for the literary portion this year is: Youth and Their Opinions. This is a broad topic and many pictures can be drawn to fit it.

The students do all the art work. Mr. Miller feels there are many promising artists here; he wishes more would participate. Many excellent pictures are now being considered for the cover.

If you're thinking of doing any art work for the ninth grade yearbook, see Mr. Miller Tuesday and Friday during afternoon homeroom. Mr. Miller would like still more of the original and exciting work he is getting.

by Debbie Brecher

```
NOTICE:

HELP MAKE

YOUR YEARBOOK

THE BEST EVER.

BRING IN

ADS AND

BOOSTER MONEY
```

Linden Reigns For Third Straight Year In Basketball

By beating Van Wyck J.H.S. 71-61 on the last day of the regular season Linden's 1968-69 cagers earned the right to enter the play-offs for the borough championship. Yes, once again Linden has rode to the top led by the coaching of the very able Mr. Trell who coached his third straight championship team this year. It was a real team effort, but if forced to pick the outstanding player this year, I would have to pick Gregory "Stick" Bierria who led the team in scoring and rebounding. (131 pts.) However, a well deserved pat on the back should go to each individual member of the team. I thought that the whole league was greatly improved this year, especially Van Wyck and Parsons J.H.S.'s, the two teams that gave us the best battles. I was greatly impressed with attendance at our home games as once again Linden's student body supported the team. Compared with the attendance that the other schools had at their games we had a mob. This year we hope to go all the way in the play-offs and it may come to pass that Linden ranks no. 1 in Queens. We'll just have to wait and see but it could very well be. Now I'd like to say congratulations to the whole team in this the third straight year that Linden has reigned over the basketball world.

```
FOR THE SCORES
OF THE PLAYOFF
GAMES SEE PAGE 2
```

```
WE ARE SORRY FOR
THE DELAY IN THIS
ISSUE. NEXT ISSUE
DUE WEEK OF 5/12
```

BOARD OF EDUCATION OF THE CITY OF NEW YORK
COMMUNITY SCHOOL DISTRICT 29

Max G. Rubinstein, Community Superintendent
Florence Friedlander, Deputy Superintendent

"PROJECT YOUTH"
Drug Abuse Prevention and Education Program
Public School 116 Annex
St. Paul's Methodist Church
173-01 108 Avenue
Jamaica 11433

Lois Samuel
Project Director

Telephone: 523-7639

January 30, 1973

Mr. William Harris, Principal
Junior High School 192
109-89 204 Street
St. Albans, New York 11412

Dear Mr. Harris:

This morning we took a group of approximately 120 students from all of the junior high schools of our district to view the PROJECT YOUTH ART EXHIBIT at the Junior Museum of the Metropolitan Museum of Art. Following this, we took the children for lunch to Howard Johnson's.

The children handled themselves with grace and dignity. They were so beautifully behaved that they received compliments not only from the restaurant staff but from patrons of the restaurant. We were very proud of them.

We congratulate you on the behavior of your students. It was a pleasure for all of us who accompanied them.

Sincerely,

Lois Samuel
Director

LS:kc

*When the museum guide explained that there was a Saturday morning children's art program and took us to where the classes were, I pointed out the room where as a requirement for my Art Education degree at City Collge, I had taught a class.
*EM note.

DISTRICT SUPERINTENDENT HONORED

l-r Ms. Jacqueline Browne, Deputy Supt. Celestine Miller. Asst. Prin. (w. corsage gift) Honoree, Ms. F. Friedlander, Community Supt., Mr. William H. Harris, Principal, 192

TEACHER RECOGNITION DAY

PTA President w. Teacher William H. Harris, Prin., w. Teacher

BOARD OF EDUCATION OF THE CITY OF NEW YORK

	Linden Jr. High School (192) Queens		
SCHOOL	BOROUGH ZONE	ADDRESS	TELEPHONE

OFFICE OF THE PRINCIPAL

November 3, 1971

Memo to Mr. Edward Miller

Dear Mr. Miller:

    Thanks for your dedicated efforts in assisting in the arrangement of our exhibit at the District Office. We are very fortunate to have personnel like yourself who are not only able to do such a fine job, but are willing to do it under extraordinary conditions and circumstances.

    Such accomplishments as this go a long way in establishing the proper image for our school.

Very sincerely yours,

William H. Harris
Principal

WHH:ML

cc: file

BOARD OF EDUCATION OF THE CITY OF NEW YORK

J.H.S. 192	Queens	11412	109-89 204th Street	479-5540
SCHOOL	BOROUGH	ZIP CODE	ADDRESS	TELEPHONE

OFFICE OF THE PRINCIPAL

June 24, 1981

Mr. Edward Miller

Dear Mr. Miller

    Thank you for your fine work in the students' lunchroom during the school year 1980-81. A well-operated and organized lunchroom is indeed a key area in the school Your efforts helped to make the lunch program a success.

    Please have a healthy and happy vacation. I look forward to working with you this coming school year in the same spirit.

Very truly yours,

Emile Germain

Surprise

The professional photographer was taking the official pictures for the yearbook and the Linden star basketball team stood ready for their shot. Everyone except the team Captain.

Suddenly he arrived straight from the shower to take his position kneeling front and center. When the pictures came back, it was noticed that everyone looked great but the Captain did not have his jock-strap on. The call came for Mr. Miller to come down to the gym ASAP!

The year following the assassination of Martin Luther King Jr., it was important to have a good memorial program as possible. Everything was carefully arranged except a picture of Dr. King I saw it was missing, provided a large poster, framed in construction paper, to the surprise of Ms. Reid and the staff. Where I found it, I have no idea but it served many programs, and even attached it to the curtain flounce beside the letters, "MARTIN LUTHER KING.

Surprise, Surprise

One term, early in my career. I received the notice that I would be teaching a social studies class. I was given a history book and instructions from the department, outlining the subject. It was ancient history about the middle east, specifically Babylon and the Mesopotamia area, now Iraq. The reason for this assignment was that the history teacher was late in getting back from a faraway trip.

Fortunately, the students were 8th grade SP, and when they entered my classroom, they were perfectly behaved. One young lady, with the most beautiful hazel sloe eyes, approached me at my desk and asked for the attendance book. "I'll take the attendance, Mr. Miller. I know all the class." What a surprise! She was proficient and made that part of the job easier.

I had not been given any books for the students, so I had prepared rexographed materials, highlights from my one book and illustrations. I inserted stories from the bible that I knew and tried to make the lesson about Hammurabi and his laws as dramatic as possible. I began to enjoy this class and the students responded to it favorably when suddenly I lost them. Many times one of them would greet me and say "Hello!" Funny, I still have those rexograph (pre-mimeograph/xerox) pages about the Tigris/Euphrates.

Je Comprende

One term, I was given an art class of Haitian students, most of whom were non-English speaking children. This came as a complete surprise but I thought with my High School French.

I could fake it. Along with the students came an elderly gentleman aide who was supposed to interpret for me. From the very beginning, this man would take a seat way in the back of the room and go to sleep. I didn't have the heart to disturb him.

Again, I was caved by a beautiful young lady who approached me and said she would help explain the lesson to the class for me. Another child helped with the attendance. With such cooperation, I was able to successfully teach the class.

I noticed that my helper took advantage of her situation and kept talking in fence to her friends throughout the class. One day, as she was passing through door, coming into the room, she was talking to the friend non-stop. A whispered to her, "Je comprendre in day best Parisian French. From then on, she behaved perfectly and made the experience perfect. In fact the art product was exceptional to the satisfaction of my supervisor.

BOARD OF EDUCATION CITY OF NEW YORK
DISTRICT-29
LINDEN JUNIOR HIGH SCHOOL - 192Q
109-89 204 STREET
ST. ALBANS, N. Y. 11412
TEL. 479-5540

MR. WILLIAM H. HARRIS
PRINCIPAL

MR. J. TRAPANI
ADMINISTRATIVE ASSISTANT

RENEE SKLAR
WILLIAM ROGER
ABRAHAM MEYER
MONA ABAEL - SCIENCE
ABRAHAM ZIPKIN - HEALTH ED.

January 10, 1972

Dear Mr. Miller:

I am writing to express my thanks and appreciation for your outstanding contribution to J.H.S. 192 during the Christmas Holiday Assemblies.

Your decorative art displays in the lobby and the auditorium enhanced the holiday atmosphere.

I look forward to the Spring Festical when we shall once again have a culminating Art Show for the pupils and the community to view.

Cordially yours,

Henrietta Berman
Assistant Principal

HB:BBM

Need To Know

One day, in one of my ordinary art classes, the one which had two single periods, I had the students do a project using pastel/chalk. This was a relatively new group of students whom I felt could be trusted with this rather messy medium. Other classes who appeared less responsible were given crayons. I explained that during the course of their work, a crayon could break, the pieces could be returned to the box for further use. The difference between an accidental breakage and an act of intentional destruction or the throwing of a piece at another student would not be tolerated. Mrs. Berman/Rosner's office next door to my room, had several chairs where I would put the miscreant, thus avoiding conflict and disruption.

All too often, not wanting to halt the work of the good students, I would overlook the pieces left around the room and collect the pieces after the class had left. Occasionally, if I caught the child in the act, I would have him do the collecting after class or see the dean. It usually worked. One such student told his father and I was summoned to Mr. Harris office. He cautioned me not to say anything when facing the irate parent.

The father began to shout accusations and I started to defend myself. The Principal signaled me by putting his finger to his lips and I stopped. He began by asking several questions of the boy, completely unrelated to me or my art room. He put the student completely on the defensive. Whereas the father began by venting his anger toward toc. be now turned it on his son. Soon the father was berating his son, getting more angry by the minute. He did not wait for the child's answer when his fist struck the boy's face. Between the child's screaming and the father's apologies, I felt sorry and guilty for what had happened.

Why that student no longer appeared in that class. I don't know and I can't hazard a guess.

However, I did learn from that time, and there were a few more times when irate parents had me called to the office, that I needed to keep my peace and allow "Counselor Harris" to proceed.

Another time, it was the second period, that the class was working with a box of pastels when a boy began violently shoving his work off the desk and throwing the pieces of pastels up into the air. He seemed to be going wild and I thought he might cause harm to other students. I cautioned the other pupils to keep working, which they obviously could not do, as I took the bay by the arms and led him out the door, where I held him firmly against the wall, telling him to stay put until I got back to him. I could not put him into Mrs. Rosner's office because she had ordered me not to do that anymore. At the bell, the students were ready to leave, had their work and the boxes of pastels collected. I told the calmed boy to get his things, to go to his next class. The next day, the student and his mother came to my room. Apparently, the whole episode had been told to her. She seemed apologetic in bar conversation "Mr. Miller, she began, "I'm sorry my boy made you trouble! He has asthma and sometimes has seizures are bad," I tried to explain that had I known, I would have gotten him help from the nurse. Why a new student's special condition is not told to his teachers is terrible. Fortunately, this time had not been too severe. I promised to look after him but it never happened again. I don't know if the mother saw anyone after she thanked me. I thought that was something I needed to know!

One term, the holiday season was approaching. This seventh grade class was clearly not prepared to create any special art work. I decided to have them make something that they could execute and make home for the Christmas holiday I took some baking home over the weekend and made a cutout Xmas Tree. When the class rived, iced the children if they would like to make a Christmas true and the response was overwhelming.

I distributed the cutout oaktag shapes the pencils and green construction paper. They folded is in half as instructed and traced the shape carefully on each side. I passed down each aisle, helping those who needed it and complimenting those who succeeded. One sweet child just sat there and did nothing. When I asked her why, she responded that she can't do it. I continued by asking if she wasn't feeling well or if there was any other reason for her abstaining.

Her friend who sat next to her explained that she was a Jehovahs Witness and she doen't believe in Christmas trees. Seeing the dilemma, I told her that she doesn't have to make a Christmas tree, that I understand. The class finished the drawing and as the work was collected, I told them that next class we will cut out the shapes and decorate them.

This situation bothered me greatly because that girl had no issue with any of the other work. The next time the class met, as promised, the safety scissors were distributed and each student cut out a pair of trees ready to be decorated with colors. I approached the Jehovah's Witnness and asked her, "I know you cannot make a Christmas tree but what about an Evergreen tree?" With the biggest, sweetest smile in the world she replied, "Yes!"

She took the oaktag shapes and drew the two evergreen shapes ready for cutting. All the others were busy decorating their trees in Christmas fashion as she finished hers, plainly. It was then the big surprise came. I took my stapler from my desk and took up her two trees, set them against each other and stapled them together. Spreading them apart at right angles, I stood her tree up on the desk in front of her and the whole class gave a round of applause. My stapler couldn't get to the other children fast enough. The homeroom teacher saw me later and told me the whole story, just as it happened. The truth is, I needed to know about the child's religion and I needed to know a solution.

CELESTINE M. REID
Administrative Assistant

BOARD OF EDUCATION   CITY OF NEW YORK

THE LINDEN SCHOOL
Office of the Principal
WILLIAM H. HARRIS
109-89 204th STREET
ST. ALBANS, NEW YORK 11412
Telephone (212) 479-5540

January 11, 1982

Mr. Edward Miller,

Dear Mr. Miller,

    Your supervision on the evening of our Winter Music Festival was most invaluable. Your presence was an indication of commitment to your profession as well as a demonstration of concern for developing good comradery.

    On behalf of the music department, thank you for volunteering. We hope that you will have a very successful new year.

Very truly yours,

Celestine V. Miller
Administrative Assistant

rld
cc:

The Little Drummer Boy

The auditorium at I.S. 192 was standing room only. Folding chairs had been set up in the isles to accommodate the excess attendance but even that was not enough. The concert was to celebrate the Christmas season and the performers were ready. The chorus and band were going to give an outstanding concert. The walls of the vestibule and auditorium were covered with the students are work and holiday decorations. The school had a festive air, appropriately, for this was a religious Black community whose culture did not separate Church and State.

The program began with the Black National Anthem, "Lift Every Voice and Sing!" The whole audience stood and sang the song. The walls shook with the applause and as soon as the audience settled down, Ms. Reid, the assistant to the Principal, rose to greet the assemblage. Although each person had a program prepared by the printing department, she never-the-less introduced the first number.

Several pieces followed with the band playing holiday themes, popular, secular songs. A medley of tunes including. "White Christmas". The chorus followed and gave an outstanding program of Gospel singing audience clapped in time to the music, many "Halleluyah's were offered and it was inspirational.

Most people never left their seat for intermission. The house lights were dimmed and the program continued. Out in front of the band stood two boys. One had a trumpet, the other a snare drum. The chorus would join them in the song. The room was electric with anticipation. The program advised them that one of the most beautiful and simple holiday tributes was to begin. The Little Drummer Boy!" Rat-a-tat, tat, repeated several times, the crescendo increasing with each round. Then the sweet, pure sound of the trumpet brought in the melody Agam building the drama with increasing volume. A few rounds and the chorus added the words, so simple a story, so moving! Up to this point, the audience was absolutely silent. Suddenly the sound of "Ooooh!" Then a burst of applause. The performers could not see what the audience did. In a slow unobtrusive movement, the solid curtain behind them gave way to an illuminated backdrop of the Three Wise Men crossing the desert below a silver star. The dramatic effect was apparent. The music went on to its dramatic conclusion. The ovation was unanimous. The curtain slowly closed over

The Drummer Boy the scene. The lamps were extinguished but not the enthusiastic response. The concert continued and ended with outstanding renditions of "Come All Ye Faithful" and the Halleluyah Chorus from Handel's Messiah. At the end of the program, when the credits were given, Mr. Miller was announced as the creator of the art work on stage. That's the end of the story.

The beginning was not as simple. Some time before, the head custodian had approached Mr. Miller with a dilemma. He was cleaning out his storage rooms and had found three rolls of transparent vinyl plastic. He didn't know how it got there or to whom it belonged. Each weighed fifty pounds and if the Art Department did not take them, he would simply dispose of them in the trash. As coordinator of the department, Mr. Miller had a stock room, so he agreed to rescue the material. The rolls were hoisted on to a rolling cart borrowed from the office. He then had to hoist them, one-by-one, up to his shoulder and carry them up one flight to his room and the store room.

Every time he needed to get something or store something, he would wonder why he had taken these bulky items that took up so much space for no apparent reason. It was months away from the holiday concert, the pale blue, the yellow and tan colored plastic had no meaning until the image of a desert scene came into his head. How to use this material, heavy gauge transparent vinyl plastic. One day, he cut some samples from the two foot high rolls. At home he experimented making overlays. By layering the blue plastic, different strata of blue sky could be made. Deeper at the top. lighter at the horizon. The perception of depth could also be achieved by layering the tan and yellow sheets into shades of yellow deepening to orange, the tan deepening to brown. Darker tones couldn't be lightened but light ones could make darker. Cutting the horizon lines into dunes, he began to create perspective and a mock-up of a scene. The vinyl was not stable as glass so it needed a support. The idea of stained-glass windows answered the question. It needed Gothic arches. He cut three arched spaces into a sheet of black construction paper, allowing for a frame all around. With scotch tape, he affixed the material to the back of the construction paper and the design came into shape. From the removed black paper, he cut out three small camels with riders to form a silhouette of figures on the dunes. The image was working visually at last.

The whole backdrop had to be light enough to hang from the flyer in front of the last the rear curtain. This covered the cinder-block wall. He had often rescued discarded appliance cartons found on the street waiting pick-up and used them for art projects. But, just when he needed a large piece, there was none. He thought of asking at a local store, but hesitated doing that. Every morning, he would turn down 111th Street, on which he usually parked near the school. This one day, for some unknown reason, he turned on to 112th street, instead. Three blocks ahead was the reason. A family had purchased a huge refrigerator-freezer and the carton was sitting on the curb. He had almost missed it then backed up and got out to examine the prize. It was perfect. No-one was around to object, so he used his utility knife to cut it make it fit into the trunk. A piece of string secured it and he slowly proceeded the few blocks to the school entrance. With the help of some students, he was able to get the cardboard into the lobby.

After parking the car and punching his time card, the find was brought up to his room. Now, the project could move forward. It would be impossible to work on it during school hours or after school. His friend, the custodian, agreed to have him work on Saturday mornings when the traffic was light and he had privacy. Being able to operate on the lobby floor was a gift. Measurements and maneuverability were essential. Some of his special students offered to assist but that was blocked by administration regulations. Besides, this was supposed to be a surprise. Several weeks passed and the layering and silhouette were stabilizing. It took some pleading and indebtedness to secure some wooden slats from the Wood Shop teacher to frame the work.

Black acrylic paint was used for the window frames and figures. A test of the mock-up on stage showed a problem. The stage lights would reflect off the glassy vinyl creating a glare. Without the stage lights, the whole thing was invisibly dark. It needed backlighting.

He had made a friend of the District Audio-Visual director who had lent him photographic equipment. A phone call, a visit and a pair of intense halogen lamps were secured. Now to call on another friend for help. His buddy art teacher, the only one in whom he had confided One afternoon, they stayed after school hours and affixed the piece to the flyer with wire. The flyer, a long pipe hanging from cables hoisted the backdrop to its appropriate height and the lamps

The Drummer Boy were set for maximum illumination. Aside from a safety factor and fire hazard, the light had to be adjusted to flood the back curtain otherwise the screen would lose its affect. It looked awesome. Position marks were set with masking tape for the lamps and the flyer. Now everything had to be secured. The lamps were allowed to cool then stored in the backstage dressing rooms. The riser was raised to put the scene out of view. The rear curtain was opened to avoid damage before the show.

The night of the concert and Mr. Miller arrived very early. He checked the artwork of the students that covered the lobby walls and the auditorium. Several hangings needed repair and the masking tape did the job. The Auditorium lights were out, so he carefully made his way to the stage and began to set up the equipment. The light from the dressing room was sufficient to plug in the lamps and adjust them. The rear curtain was closed and the flyer lowered. The halogen lamps were lit and the test proved there need a slight adjustment. Then they were put off and the outer rear curtain was closed so the scene was hidden. All he had to do was wait for the night time.

Mr. Miller, the ex-officio yearbook photographer went to his room to dress for the evening and get his camera. His buddy, the Art Teacher/MC Mr. Gadson, in his tuxedo, was checking out the program They decided that the right moment was during the "Little Drummer Boy At the agreed signal, they both disappeared behind the stage, lit the lamps hidden from the audience and slowly opened the inner curtain exposing the illuminated scene.

The Principal and his assistant congratulated Mr. Miller as did members of the audience. The following day, the student body would be treated to the program and the Little Drummer Boy showing. The lamps were returned the scenery stayed on the flyer until it could be salvaged.

The student's art work was removed after a week to keep it from destruction and returned to them at teras end as promised Mr. Miller was asked to make another backdrop for the next program. He declined. Perhaps something else, something different would happen, and it did.

Becomes of a Tuba

Whether it is coincidence, irony or fate, I'm not sure but whatever it is, there is undoubtedly something strange in this set of circumstances. It is a problem where and how to begin. For many years, as an Art teacher at the Linden School, LS 192Q, in a predominantly black community serving St. Albans, Cambria Heights and Hollis, Queens, I was interested and involved in the civil rights struggle of the African-American people but this was not something new to my life experience. In the course of my work, I was able to circumvent the obsolete official Board of Education art curriculum and my Assistant Principal's instructions, to institute my own programs. This allowed a wide range of experience, skills and subjects in the special classes. They were called, "Talent Class". The majority of my students opted to be in the ART program. Other classes to choose from were Choral Singing, Band, Dance and various shops.

When I began teaching at LS 192, it was as a substitute. I replaced an art teacher who was on sabbatical leave. I was given her special, responsible job of "coordinator" which involved ordering supplies, dispensing paper and materials to the other four Art teachers and acting as liaison between them and the A.P. The job also meant getting orders from the school administration to the art department. Every term, I had to prepare a portfolio of students' work to decorate the Superintendent's district office. When the special classes' projects, which included African masks, wood carving, found object sculpture, paper mache, construction paper work, clay figures of three and two dimensional design were successfully completed, I would decorate two of four large showcases in the hallway of the art wing.

The other art teachers periodically changed the display with the projects of their own. When the Spring and Winter Music festivals were performed, I helped coordinate the decorating of the lobby and interior walls of the assembly hall with all the students' artwork. These mostly related to the season or subjects of current interest. One such project had different illustrations for Alex Halley's "Roots!" which were inspired from the reading of the book as well as seeing the TV presentation. One year, many students made a 4 foot by 8 foot mural depicting the heroic leaders of Black history. It was drawn on cardboard in pastels, framed and hung in the lobby of the school. During the '60s and '70s many assembly programs were held on the struggles in the South and on one occasion, I designed a black construction-paper silhouette stage design for a dramatization backdrop. It included a three part depiction, of Dr. King in the center with the sit-in to the left and the bus boycott to the right. This image, as a triptych re-rained in my mind, waiting for the right time to develop it into a full color mural And that time arrived because of a tuba.

Will Bush, was a senior at the time, had requested admission to the band talent class of C. I. Williams, a music teacher and professional saxophone player with excellent credentials. The student had excellent credentials also, had skills in many instruments, ability in writing scores and had his own jazz band. Not only was he musically creative and talented but he was an "A" student also. So, when the tuba, a not very inspiring instrument, was made available to him, he was very disappointed and decided to take the Art talent class instead. The only opening in that time slot was my class. My first inclination was to be wary, as he was possibly a reject from the Band class because of a disciplinary problem, which was not uncommon. Much to my surprise, he completed.

Civil Rights Triptych c.'81
Student/Artist: Will Bush
Art Teacher: Ed Miller
Acrylic Ptg. - Masonite 4'x8'
"Because of a Tuba!"

The gesso was dry, the drawing enlarged and copied onto the Masonite. The painting began to appear. It took some persuading to keep the class from stopping their own work to watch Will at his. In fact he was so eager that he urged his other teachers to excuse him so that he could work on the masterpiece.

He would often stay after school to paint so as not to feel self-conscious in front of the other kids. Of course this was his job and he was exempt from the other art assignments. On occasion, he did need some advice, deciding on colors or mixing paints and I was only too happy to make suggestions, giving him alternatives. What had begun in the cool of winter, had stretched into the hot of early May and June. The call of the outdoors became strong and it took some persuasion to keep the young artist at his work. His urging me to finish it for was rejected out of hand. It was his baby, after all Although, I had thought to keep the work in progress from the administration, the assistant to the Principal happened by and got to see it. Soon we were visited by the Principal who was very impressed. I took advantage of the moment to suggest that a suitable frame would be needed and to hint where it would look well mounted in the lobby. The assurances were made but getting the job done was running into trouble.

Will was preparing for graduation, with honors and his interest in completing the mural began to wane. Rehearsals took precedence over art class. The question of touching up a spot here or there, finishing the edging was beyond his patience, A little cajoling finally got him to finish the masterpiece. His last act was to put his name at the bottom. He was not as happy as I was when I congratulated him upon its completion. A final step had to be done. I could not ask him to cover the mural with several coatings of protective varnish, so I had to add the finishing touch. Then I realized that the frame would cover his name but I decided to let it go. Finally, after many requests and getting the Principal's help, the mural was framed and bolted to the wall in the lobby. I had to use a marker pen to rewrite Will Bush's name on the bottom left, above the frame and my own at the right. There the dream, the triptych remains for all to see. For some unknown reason, with the oncoming month of February and the celebration of Black History month 1998, I was inspired to write a poem about my dream. It was to be about a triptych mural and how I had been waiting for that one special student. It was a strange coincidence, that several years later, during Black History month, C.I. Williams, passed on. The teacher who had offered Will Bush the tube and unknowingly sent the artist to me. The triptych mural came to life not because of Will Bush, me or C.I. Williams but because of a tuba.

CIVIL RIGHTS MURAL 4'x8' IS 192Q

s, voice lessons, and piano lessons in Pine Bush, New York...   http://www.learningmusician.com/

LearningMusician
power tools for teachers and students

 Find a Teacher   Find Students   Help   About Us

Home   Join   Articles   Forums   Browse Teachers   Teachers' Guide

William Bush

Offering private lessons in Pine Bush, New York

About Me   **Contact Me**

Introduction
I am a professional musician/producer/songwriter/teacher with years of teaching and performing experience. I Offer lessons for piano/keyboards, guitar, bass, drums and voice for all ages. Theory classes and band workshops are also available.

My Teaching Background
I have been a professional musician since high school. I attended the Brooklyn Conservatory of Music and studied under Enos Payne. I have performed and recorded with many major label artists since 1989. I have recorded with Aretha Franklin, Anita Baker, Christina Aguilera, Tupac Shakur and many others. I have several platinum awards and one Grammy nomination. I found that while working for newer recording artists, I spent a lot of time teaching them what I knew about music and enjoying the fact that I was making a difference in their careers. I finally took the next step and began teaching privately in 2002. I also taught at the Queens Village School of Music in Queens NY. After relocating to the Hudson valley, I continued developing my own roster of students and in 2006 founded the Pine Bush School of Rock where I specialize in helping students to discover just how enjoyable playing music can be. Whether it's rock or classics, playing an instrument will stay with students for the rest of their lives if they choose to keep playing. I love being a part of that process.

I have also been a music consultant for the poughkeepsie school system since 2004. I currently give lectures and demonstrations for music production and music business at the New School for Radio and Television in Albany NY. I also teach recording classes for the Newburgh Performing Arts Academy. I am currently doing production work for independent artists. The latest project landed at #42 on the Billboard Jazz chart in late 2011.

My Teaching Philosophy
I find out why my student wants to play music. Then I create a lesson/study plan that will help the student achieve exactly that. I try to give as much background as possible when teaching. I want my students to be good musicians and not just be able to play music.

All I need from a student is a willingness to learn. If a student is willing to learn then the sky is the limit. As students gain more confidence and skill, I offer performance opportunities of all types such as; recitals, concerts,gigs, television shows, etc. These opportunities will coincide with the student's personal goals and desires.

Rates And Availability
I charge $40/hr lesson or $30/half hr. lesson. I teach Mon.- Thur. at my home studio in Pine Bush NY.

As a matter of fact, since receiving your letter, I have been finding myself sketching little scenes here and there. I have some canvas that I have been saving for just the right image. I just need to find something that really moves me.

I would like for you to know that you had a very positive effect on my life and I am grateful for our time together. Your letter meant a lot to me and it came at a perfect time as well. Thank you.

6-31-2015

Excerpt above from letter recieved 30 years after William's graduation/ completion of the Civil Rights Mural

E.M.

Sincerely yours,

William Bush

William Bush

I offer lessons in:
- Adult Piano Methods
- Arranging
- Audio Engineering
- Audio Production
- Pop Bass
- Rock Bass
- Funk / R&B Bass
- Children's Piano Methods
- Composition
- Rock Drums
- Ear Training
- Acoustic Guitar
- Electric / Rock Guitar
- Improvisation
- Contemporary Christian Keyboard
- Pop / Rock Keyboard
- Music History
- Basic Music Theory
- Intermediate Music Theory
- Advanced Music Theory
- Jazz Organ
- Rock Organ
- Jazz Piano
- Popular Piano
- Songwriting
- Pop Voice
- R&B / Hip-Hop Voice
- Rock Voice

Interested in taking lessons with William?

Click the button below to send a private message.

Send Message

Site design,framework, and original content copyright 2005-2015 by LearningMusician.com a division of Empty Sea Productions, LLC

GYM

THE HARLEM WIZARDS

"Mr. Miller," the message that I received read. "Please come to the gym right away with your camera! A substitute will cover you." Signed Miss Reid. It was the third period and the class was involved in a special project and they were special children, so I knew there would be no problem. They understood my reason and left. The job was a big and wonderful surprise. The Harlem Wizards (like the Globetrotters) put on a fabulous show!

BOARD OF EDUCATION OF THE CITY OF NEW YORK

J.H.S. 192	Queens 11412	109-89 204th St.	479-5540
SCHOOL	BOROUGH ZONE	ADDRESS	TELEPHONE

OFFICE OF THE PRINCIPAL

June 16, 1982

Mr. E. Miller

Dear Mr. Miller:

    The contributions that you make to the school's special activities and yearbook are of such significance that we want to express our gratitude.

    Your demonstration of committment to your photography which is all done on your time is an indication of professionalism and support of the administration's goals and objectives.

    The decorations that you along with many youngsters displayed for the prom on Friday, June 11 were a beauty and joy to behold. I realize that this is an assignment that is normally done by another art teacher who was on leave at the time. Without my suggesting to you that this assignment had to be completed, you showed the initiative that this administration has made an effort to instill in each of our staff. Your keen sensitivity to the needs of the school, your following through on all directions relative to the school's operation without reminder show professional maturity.

    I wish you much success in all of your future endeavors. You are a great photographer. Thanks for capturing all of the poignant moments that we can all relive over the past 12 years.

Very truly yours,

Celestine V. Miller
Acting Principal

AKA Ms. Reid

cc: File

BOARD OF EDUCATION OF THE CITY OF NEW YORK

SCHOOL	BOROUGH ZONE	ADDRESS	TELEPHONE
	Linden Jr.H.S. (192)		

OFFICE OF THE PRINCIPAL

June 15, 1972

Memo to Mr. E. Miller

Dear Mr. Miller:

    Thank you for giving up your time and expending the effort to assist us in making our graduation prom a success for the pupils. I must say that it was one of the most successful proms that I have ever witnessed, and I ʃ am deeply grateful and appreciative to you for your assistance in helping us to do this.

    Such cooperation as this will finally help us attain our main objective, and that is to have Linden become one of the best schools in the city.

    Thanking you again, I am

                              Very sincerely,

                              William H. Harris
                              Principal

Mr. Jorif, A.P. escorts

two beautiful graduates

at Linden prom.

The End Term Party

There was no official invitation, just a phone call. The voice, very sweet and of course, apologetic. "How could we overlook you? You're our favorite, you know it!" Ms. Doby, her beautiful smile evident in her voice. Actually, I had been on sick leave since April, because of a bad back, but many of my acquaintances and friends hadn't noticed my absence. The fact that the year before I had been on sabbatical made the oversight understandable. Many teachers disappeared from our school without a trace when they would leave for greener pastures. The last day of the term coincided with my retirement, having served twenty years and reached my 62nd birthday, and according to the UFT contract.

The party was held in a local hall and the place was beautifully decorated. When my wife and I arrived, we were greeted with hugs and kisses. A white carnation was fixed to my lapel and we were escorted over to the VIP table. So many of the staff came over with cordial greetings. The teachers who only knew me only when they needed my help or art materials, made no attempt to visit. A member of the cafeteria staff was also being honored for her years of service and retirement. The Principal was very kind in his expression of regret at losing me.

He had neglected saving a copy of the yearbook for me. Assistant Principal, Mr. Jorif offered his copy and I appreciated the kindness. It would complete the set of yearbooks that I had collected since teaching at Linden.

The room soon filled with the people whom I worked with and befriended over the twenty years. There were some new faces who were introduced to me, including the art teacher who covered for me in my absence. Best of all, was the attendance of our former principal and assistant to the principal who had moved on, before. The cocktails flowed freely and the buffet dinner was excellent. The current principal gave a stirring speech, lauding his people for another superior year. He was very generous in recognizing the 120% effort that I had contributed to the students and the school. The applause from the guests was generous, also.

After several other speakers, The End Term Party hostess invited Ms. Gordon and me to the dais. A bouquet of roses was presented to the woman and brass clock/barometer/thermometer was given to me. The gift box was sealed and the audience chanted for me to open it. The call then came for a speech. It took several minutes to collect my thoughts and take the paper from my pocket. Then I said, "Thank you all for the party and the happy twenty years at Linden." I waited for the laughter to subside. After some pertinent remarks, I concluded with, "I hope you will miss me as much as I will miss all of you! Whenever you enter the lobby, I hope the Civil Rights mural that Will Bush made, will remind you of this art teacher." Then I held up the clock. "For this, thanks! The clock will remind me to get up for work. The barometer will tell me the weather is too lousy, the thermometer, too cold to get up and I'll turn over and go back to sleep! Thank you!"

My speech was well received and the applause will receive. However, what was in my heart was not to be said. My sabbatical was taken the year before my retirement, on purpose. In the year that I was away, the art program was eliminated, doing away with specialized double classes. Whatever materials that I had left in my supply closet were gone. The art funding minimalized so no special projects were possible. The student's attitude was, "This is a minor subject and unimportant. My sciatica back pain was severely acting up, so I had to finish my teaching career using up my sick leave, to the day. I still had all the happy years to remember.

The Reunion

The crowd of guests had arranged themselves in clusters of four or five around the hall.

It was sort of a reunion, well for some, although many of the men and women had been friends for years since they attended school together. The gentle murmur of the conversation showed a warmth and comradery that made the reunion a success.

A former student, Johnny moved easily from one group to another. His warm, engaging smile and twinkling eyes, set in his ebony face matched well with his deep baritone voice.

"Hi!" he said, as he entered this small group of young men and women standing a little way from the bar.

"Hi! My name is Mary Jay!" the pretty young lady said as the reached her hand toward the one that Johnny extended. Hers was cold from the fresh highball she was holding. The high school streamers and balloons made a festive ballroom out of the basketball court gymnasium of the junior high school that they had attended many years ago. "I'm sorry, but I seem to have forgotten your name!" she said.

"I'm Johnny Jeffereson, class of 78," he replied, scanning the faces of the men and women in the tight circle. "I hope that I'm not interrupting anything." He paused to check the faces of the others. "Let's see, I came to Linden in 76, when Dr. Fox was principal, I think."

Joseph, a heavy-set five foot eleven, in a loud plaid sports jacket, laughed. "What's the difference, anyhow? Welcome anyway!" Everyone smiled warmly. I just stood there patiently waiting for the introductions to go around. Mary Jay did the honors. "Johnny, this is Lisa, Jamal, Damen, and Mabel and Joseph. And this is Mr. Millar, our art teacher, whom you probably remember. Each same followed with a warm handshake and an even warmer smile.

The teacher, who had retired long before, cleared his throat sad remarked, "To tell the truth, you'll have to forgive me not remembering your names, but your face all ring a bell. I'll just have to downsize all of you to age thirteen and fourteen, so please be patient with me."

Damon held up his hand as though he was still back in the classroom. "There's something in the back of my memory," and a funny glint came into his hazel eyes as he recalled what had happened. "One day as Mr. Miller was returning from the hallway, he caught me smoking a cigarette in the coat closet."

Lisa gasped. The young lady still had that baby face with those aloe eyes that made her so charming. "What a dumb thing to do!" she interrupted.

Jamal agreed! "It sure was stupid, man, and a good thing Mr. Man caught you before you set fire to the school and my leather in that closet."

Damon continued. "I was sure he was going to turn me over to the dean and I would have had to bring up my mom and everything."

"Well, what happened?" Mary Jay asked, impatiently.

Damon continued. "Instead of turning me in, he took me aside and quietly asked me to give him the box of Marlboros."

Mabel turned to Mr. Miller and asked, "Why didn't you report him? After all, he did something dangerous, didn't he?"

"Well," Damon answered, "I really expected all hell to break loose. He took a gamble, and his instinct was right. When I surrender my cigarettes, he spoke to me in a nice tone and did what he promised. He said he'd give them back at 3:00 o'clock. Then he did give them back after school. No other teacher ever kept his word as you did, sir. Mr. Miller, you gave me several choices, cooperate and do well in class, no smoking in school, or get turned in."

Mary Jay recalled, "Wasn't Damon one of your best pupils? Didn't he win an art reward from Lever Brothers and his work on the yearbook?"

Mr. Miller and I had a deal and it worked. You should have seen how proud he was when I came up in my Navy uniform after I enlisted. I may have grown up but still haven't kicked the habit!"

Joseph said, "Let's drink to that!" and they all raised their glasses.

While the conversation was going on, a tall thin young man joined the group and waited for a break to introduce himself. "I'm Andy..."

Before he could say his last name everyone chimed in, "Andy, Andy Russel!" And who wouldn't remember him, the star of Linden's basketball team. Andy had a ginger ale in his hand because of a drinking problem. "I also have a story to tell." he began as everyone eagerly waited on his every word. They were sure he was going to tell a basketball story, but that wasn't it.

"Do you guys remember," he began, "how during the watercolor class, Mr. Miller used to repeat over and over, don't flood the pigment!" and how excited he became if one of us put in too much water? When it finally sunk in that he was right, the paint would get all used up and we would get upset when the pigment disappeared."

"Sure we remember. So what?" asked Joseph

"Hush!" said Lisa, her bright smile belying her curt remark. "Let him tell it!"

"Coming home from Andrew Jackson high school one day, at three o'clock with say buddies, we were passing Linden, when we saw Mr. Miller across the street going to his car. I don't know if he saw my struggling but I just couldn't remember his name No matter how hard, nothing came up. All of a sudden, I hollered out, "Don't Flood The Pigment! Then you red and waved, the smile you gave was so cool! When I got home, I looked it up in the yearbook I may forget it but not, "Don't Flood The Pigment!"

I couldn't speak for a few minutes, being overwhelmed with emotion. "That's the best story: I've ever heard! Thank you!" I said,

"What & terrific story!" everyone agreed "It's so funny!"

As everyone sipped their drinks, thinking about the conversation, I thought to himself, how plaques, medals and awards are great rewards, recognition from your peers is tremendous.

"Has anyone seen Will Bush, the Civil Rights artist? Mr. Miller inquired.

"I was told that his beautiful triptych has been removed from the lobby and was replaced by a gandy revolving electric sign saying, "WELCOME PARENTS!" said Johnay. I was shocked when I visited my nephew's class. Linden has become half Elementary school."

"How criminal! That was a masterpiece that took him all term to paint the three scenes with Woolworth on the left, Martin Luther King in the middle and Rosa Parks on the right. We were all so proud of it!" Roger complained.

Unobtrusively, the lovely Carol Waite arrived late in the crowd. "She is the young lady who gave me a gift, a painting she did of a Balinese dancer. As he shook her both hands, he explained how much that picture is treasured to this day.

"I also have the woolen hooked rug, brown bear that Regina, in my special ed class made for me. She said for me stopping the others from bullying her in the art class. Apparently, she's not here, today?"

"What about the coffee mug souvenir that I brought you from my Philadelphia trip? You didn't think I wanted you to keep it, did you?" reminded Lisa.

"Do any of you remember the day that we were caught 'Break Dancing in the back of the art room?" Henry began. "You tell it, Mr. Miller".

"No! Why don't you, Henry?" I suggested.

"Well, Mr. Miller was returning from hall duty when he caught a few of us doing our thing. We had shoved the tables and chairs aside and there we were spinning and leaping with all the other students cheering and clapping. We thought that you would give us hell when you caught us but instead you complimented our skill."

"You were great!" I interrupted "But I had to get the room in order before Mrs. Roser, the A.P. next door found out. I did allow time after the lesson for you guys to continue. It was dangerous, but I took a chance, you guys were so good. When I tipped off the gym department, you saw what happened. The next concert you became performance 'stars!'"

As I was finishing, a sweet young lady came over and kissed me on the check. "Remember me?" Natalie cooed. "You made me an artist!" A professional artist and a teacher. I could see that the honorees were going to the head table and so I told the people we have to break it up.

The host announced for everyone to take their seats and we sadly separated, promising to exchange our contact information before we left. The guests of honor were introduced to resounding applause. Speeches and acknowledgement were made and the honorees were awarded trophies. I joined the members of the Linden staff at the dais and gave a small recognition speech. Actually, my heart was so full of joy that my words hardly came out. This was something that never happened in room 212.

When the band began to play, Ms. Allen asked me to dance. It was determined that I was a better art teacher than a dancer. Such an occasion can only be realized once in a lifetime. If only one is blessed with such a life, such pupils in such a school.

Approval?

One of my favorite students paused as he entered the room. He reached up to touch the temple of my forehead. "Where are your hors?" he asked.

"Horns?" I said. Of course I understood that he must have heard in church that Jews had had, "I have no horns!"

"Oh! I know! You're able to retract them. You're bad, Mr. Miller!"

He went on to his seat leaving me utterly confused for this was a boy with whom I had a cordial relationship. Why would he say that I was bad?

A different time, another boy on passing into the classroom said, "You a homeboy!"

This too was confusing in that he would call me 'boy'.

I tried to forget these expressions but it just seemed to bother me until I found out that "BAD" meant good, not bad and homeboy meant pal or buddy. Both expression of approval.

What greater indication of appreciation is there than a student giving the teacher a gift. When the young lady brought the beautifully decorated coffee mug from a family trip to Philadelphia, I acknowledged it and commented on the artwork, and handed it back to her. What a surprise it was when she said it was for me, and it sits prominently in my showcase.

When Carol Waite showed me the framed painting she had made of a Balinese dancer, I praised it for its beauty and she gave it to me, where it decorates the foyer in my home.

Charles Delaney and Curtis Ramsey presented me with their work that they did at home. All their gifts were unexpected and still treasured 40 years later.

Upon graduation, many of my students asked me to autograph their yearbooks Only my twin girls, Maria and Michele gave their graduation photo. Which former students living in my building or neighborhood point me out to friends or family as their art teacher it is so gratifying.

Sometime after retirement a young lady got in touch with me and sent me tickets to an art show in the Javits Center in New York. My wife and I couldn't wait to meet one of my prize pupils. Natalie Alleyne and see her work. Over the years, she has pursued her career as a teacher and professional artist in African themes in all media with great pride! During our luncheon in the diner, she showed us the magnificent work she was producing, all in the African realm. Her jeweled masks and powerfully dramatic cultural themes were outstanding and bringing in good prices at the many arts shows she holds around the country as well as Africa. Her headdress was an indication that she was becoming a Nigerian priestess as well as artist.

Maria Chimienti   Michele Chimienti

At Alleyne Studio, New Jersey   At AAA Diner, Queens

GIFT ART

HOOK RUG

S E Childs Name Unknown!

In an art-Special Ed Class
There was a timid child
Harassed by another boy and girl
Who nearly drove her wild.

"Such intolerable behavior…"
The teacher stopped it cold
"We behave in art class!"
The pupils were sternly told.

The week before the holiday
She gave the teacher a hug
Sha had brought him a present
A 14x18 inch plush hook rug.

"Did your mother make it?"
"No! I did it!" came her reply
"I want you to have it teacher!"
Then came the reason why.

Read at B & N Freash Meadows

CAROL WAITE

"You wouldn't let the bullies
Treat me so very bad.
Say nasty hateful things
That make me feel so sad!"

The beautiful Teddy bear nug
Into my closet, put it away
In case the sweet child's mother
Would come for it some day.

In June, I took the present home
To hang with my works of an
One of my many treasures
Given me from the heart.

Every day I think of her
Asl see the Teddy bear
À sample child's present
A treasure oh so dear.

Excerpt from "Rhymes and Reasmo" III

Al Carrion

Charles E. Delaney

Charles E. Delaney

Curtis Ramsey

Office of the Principal
MARTIN A. DREW

BOARD OF EDUCATION
CITY OF NEW YORK

THE LINDEN SCHOOL JUNIOR HIGH SCHOOL 192
109-89 204th STREET
ST. ALBANS, NEW YORK 11412
Telephone (212) 479-5540

October 6, 1983

Mr. Edward Miller

Dear Mr. Miller:

    Many thanks for this beautiful collage that you prepared for my office. This magnificent work of art truly is a masterpiece. With all of its symmetry and precision, I am sure that it took hours of careful planning and arranging to piece together all of these photographs which tell the story of my first year here at Linden.

    I shall cherish this item for years to come. As I look upon it, I shall remember all of the beautiful times that I shared with the staff and students during the school year 1982-83. This will be possible for me now that you have so creatively made an official record of these recollections.

    Thanks for making this possible.

                              Sincerely,

                              MARTIN DREW
lm   Principal

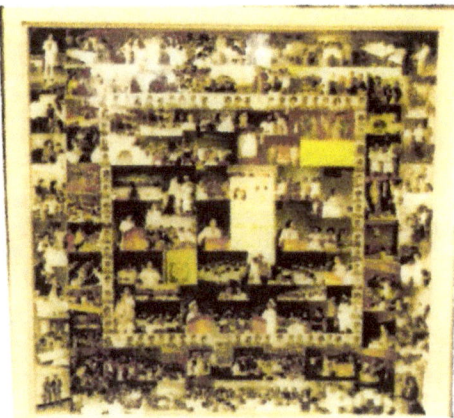

LIZA AND LISA

(Inspired Fiction)
Illustration for Liza and Lisa

Not only did the sisters in my 7th and 8th grade Art Talent class have similar names but they were genetically identical twins. Not just identical but EYEDENTICAL. and I could not tell them apart. They were excellent students, courteous, helpful, intelligent and talented. Even after twenty years they are often on my mind. My effort to find them in the phone directory failed, and I never expected to see them again.

Last week, after visiting a relative at North Shore, LIJ Hospital, I was waiting for the elevator when a sweet voice behind me asked, "Mr. Miller?" The crowd of people made it difficult to turn around, so I pretended not to have heard; after all, I could have been mistaken.

The question was repeated, only this time the voice came from a tall, lovely young woman in a nurse's uniform who had hold of my arm. Instantaneously, I recognized that it was one of the Estrella twins, but was it Liza or Lisa?

She stood next to me in the elevator. "Mr. Miller," she whispered, "don't you remember me?" Timidly, I whispered back, "Sure I do!" trying to hide my inner turmoil as to which twin this was. How often did I suffer this feeling so long ago when they were in my Art Talent Class?

"I'm going to the cafeteria, Please join me for coffee," she pleaded.

Except for a few of the personnel and us, the elevator emptied out at the main floor. As we walked down the corridor she got on the cell phone. "Hon! Meet me in the cafe! I have a surprise for you!"

After twenty years, she was still playing their tricks on me. She had called her sister "Hon!"

not giving me a clue to her identity. The name tag on her blouse read Estrella, nothing else. Her I.D. was conveniently reversed, also keeping me from that information. Was this intentional?

As children they had delighted in fooling me by switching seats. I had tried to devise a system to seat the pupils alphabetically, to make it simpler to distribute their work and to help me remember their names, to identify them. Although each class only had 30 students, my ten different classes added up to 300. I had no difficulty in remembering the Estrella twins, I only had trouble knowing which was which.

While we waited, we engaged in small talk. No, neither was married. Her parents were fine. They were no longer in the Queens phone directory. She lived in Manhattan, her sister, in Scarsdale with her man. Suddenly, a tall stately young woman approached. I stood up to greet the other half of the Estrella twins. In a mocking tone, the nurse introduced us. "Mr. Miller, meet Dr. Estrella, Pediatrician" Before I knew it, the Doctor's arms enveloped me, the stethoscope pressing into my chest. When I pulled back, I could see the big smile on her face. I had to hold back my tears.

"Dr. Lisa!" I cried. "Wow! I am overwhelmed!" I leaned over to her sister and kissed her cheek. "Lize! You were always the devilish one! How could I ever forget you guys? You were always helpful as monitors. You were so sympathetic when the trouble makers disrupted the lesson and I lost my cool. Remember the little Christmas gifts I was not allowed to take, that you would hide in my desk?"

"That was Lisa's idea! The heart of gold!"

"Mr. Miller," Lisa interrupted. "Did you notice the paintings around the cafeteria? Check them out before you leave. Remember how you insisted that we sign our pictures and include the date? Every time we finished a painting, we thought of you" Liza smiled in agreement "Kids!" I began, then caught myself.

"That's O.K.!" they replied in unison.

"Anyway, what I wanted to say was that you girls were the only students to give me their graduation pictures when I signed the yearbooks."

Liza went to the counter and brought back our coffee and Danish. The conversation flowed with reminiscences of those days at I.S.1920; interspersed with questions about the time since then.

They recalled how they were able to trick me by switching seats and bow I tried to thwart them by having Liza sit behind Lisa instead of next to her. They laughed at the fact that they fooled me anyway. They were still the adorable people I had grown to love. The clock signaled that they had to get back to the job. I thanked them with hugs and kisses. In all the excitement, I forgot to get their current addresses and phone numbers. As they said good-by and left, Liza asked, "How did you know which one we were?"

In Closing

For those who journeyed through this adventure with me, it should be clear that I was a very lucky teacher. From the inception, I was given many jobs, not just in the classroom but throughout the district. Never in my wildest dreams would I have thought of meeting people from my childhood on the front steps of an elementary school I was assigned to visit. One was Bette Endlich, teacher, my sister's close friend and another time the nemesis/bully of my junior high school life, Paul Shaeffer, ironically, an attendance officer.

Shortly after beginning this job, we were involved in organizing our school into the UFT. The parents in the neighborhood were angry with us being on the picket line and several local teachers passed through. One mother was especially vocal in berating us. After we won and went back to work, this woman whose kids were in my class became a classroom aid and pursued her college degree, becoming a teacher, alongside us. How apologetic she became, as realized how vital the union was and joined us.

In time program was adjusted so that my free periods allowed me to take care of outside business before classes some days and after classes other days. After several years, I had no need to punch the time clock, in or out. This freed me up to take care of visits to the district office when requested. I also had a working relationship with the engineering department, at a school in a different neighborhood, allowing me to get electrical materials for special assembly programs. In order to supply Mr. Gadson with pictures for the yearbook, I had to bring in the film on my last period and pick up the photos in the first.

My effort to keep in touch with former pupils and associates has been rewarding but not as much as I would wish. Will Bush wrote from upstate New York that his first love, music, has become his successful profession. Natalie Alleyne, in New Jersey, professional artist, you have seen. Ms. Reid/Miller/Harris is in touch from South Carolina, Mr. Jorif, from Florida and student Carol Waite, from Michigan. Other efforts such as Al Carrion, the Chimienti twins have failed. Many former pupils are my neighbors. Too many dear friends are reported gone, Mr. Feinstien, Mr. Meyer, Mr. Harris.

One cannot express more vigorously than in these words and these pictures the great love this teacher has for the wonderful opportunity given to me for those years in The Linden School.

L.S. 1920, District 29, Board of Education with a wonderful staff and more wonderful children.

In Closing

For those who journeyed through this adventure with me, it should be clear that I was a very lucky teacher. From the inception, I was given many jobs, not just in the classroom but throughout the district. Never in my wildest dreams would I have thought of meeting people from my childhood on the front steps of an elementary school I was assigned to visit. One was Bette Endlich, teacher, my sister's close friend and another time the nemesis/bully of my junior high school life, Paul Shaeffer, ironically, an attendance officer.

Shortly after beginning this job, we were involved in organizing our school into the UFT. The parents in the neighborhood were angry with us being on the picket line and several local teachers passed through. One mother was especially vocal in berating us. After we won and went back to work, this woman whose kids were in my class became a classroom aid and pursued her college degree, becoming a teacher, alongside us. How apologetic she became, as realized how vital the union was and joined us.

In time program was adjusted so that my free periods allowed me to take care of outside business before classes some days and after classes other days. After several years, I had no need to punch the time clock, in or out. This freed me up to take care of visits to the district office when requested. I also had a working relationship with the engineering department, at a school in a different neighborhood, allowing me to get electrical materials for special assembly programs. In order to supply Mr. Gadson with pictures for the yearbook, I had to bring in the film on my last period and pick up the photos in the first.

My effort to keep in touch with former pupils and associates has been rewarding but not as much as I would wish. Will Bush wrote from upstate New York that his first love, music, has become his successful profession. Natalie Alleyne, in New Jersey, professional artist, you have seen. Ms. Reid/Miller/Harris is in touch from South Carolina, Mr. Jorif, from Florida and student Carol Waite, from Michigan. Other efforts such as Al Carrion, the Chimienti twins have failed. Many former pupils are my neighbors. Too many dear friends are reported gone, Mr. Feinstien, Mr. Meyer, Mr. Harris.

One cannot express more vigorously than in these words and these pictures the great love this teacher has for the wonderful opportunity given to me for those years in The Linden School.

L.S. 1920, District 29, Board of Education with a wonderful staff and more wonderful children.

IN CONCLUSION

Dear reader, whoever you may be, relative, associate, friend! Hopefully, you have actually read this book, and enjoyed it too. This is but another small record of a portion of my life and time.

So many of the letters in my file were omitted due to repetition, or dealt with principal's and A.P.'s observations of a classroom procedure, or another duty which could not be illustrated easily.

Also omitted were some unfortunate occasions which are of a negative nature. unworthy of this teacher's exposing you too.

Finally, most important, the conclusion that you the reader has arrived at, after meeting this array of children and adults at 192.

Ed Miller, Author

www.ingramcontent.com/pod-product-compliance
Lightning Source LLC
LaVergne TN
LVHW071656060526
838201LV00037B/363